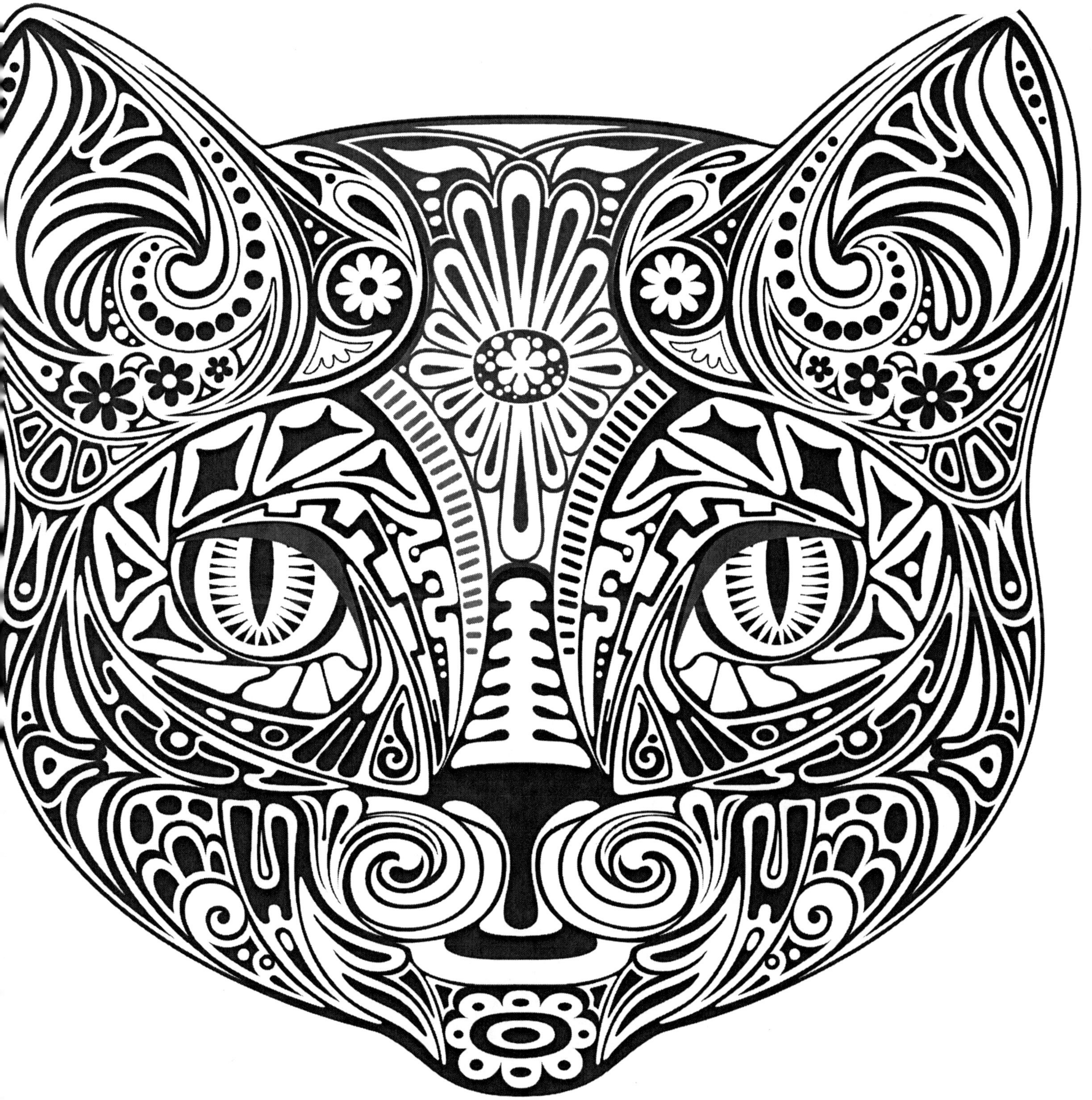

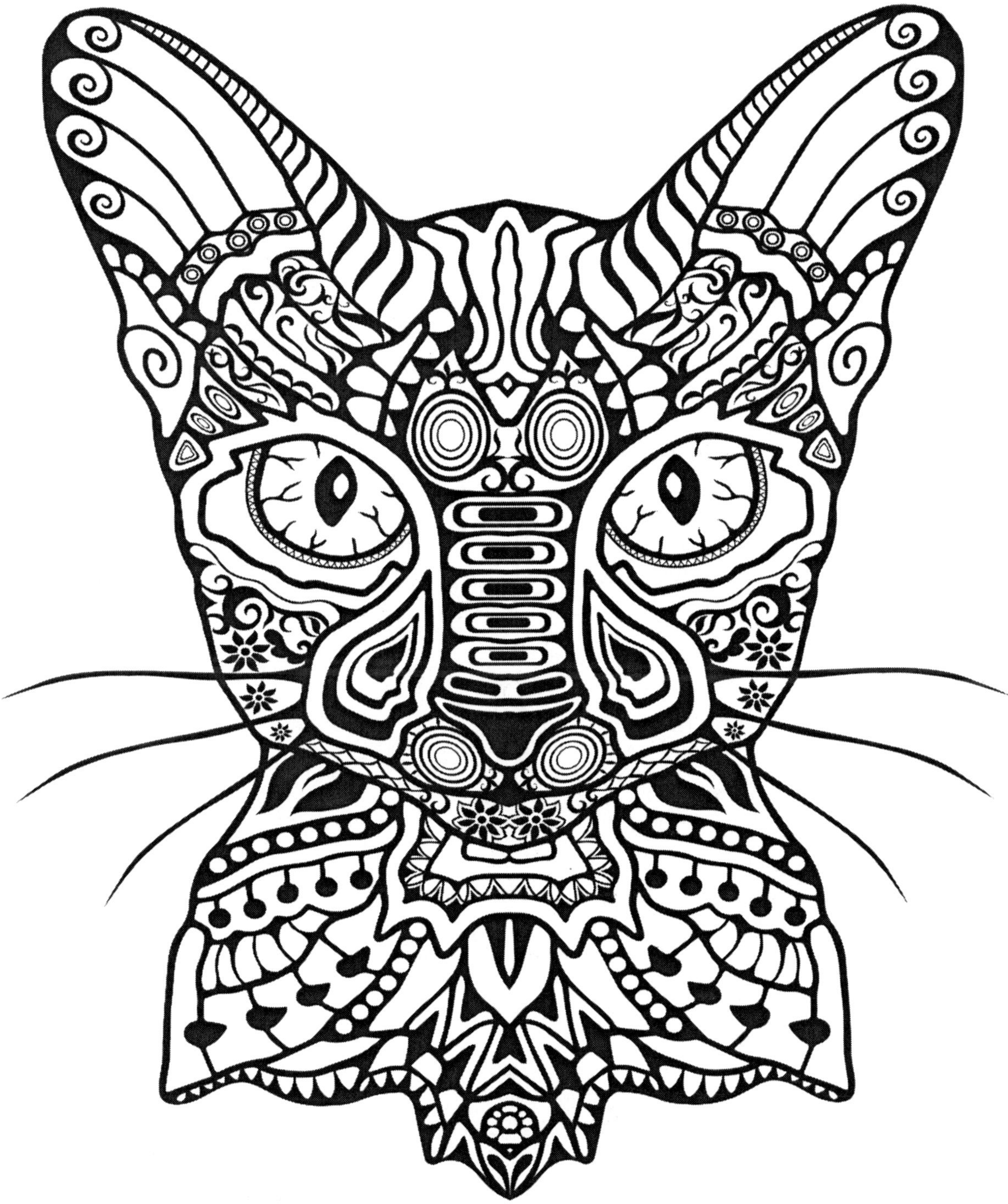

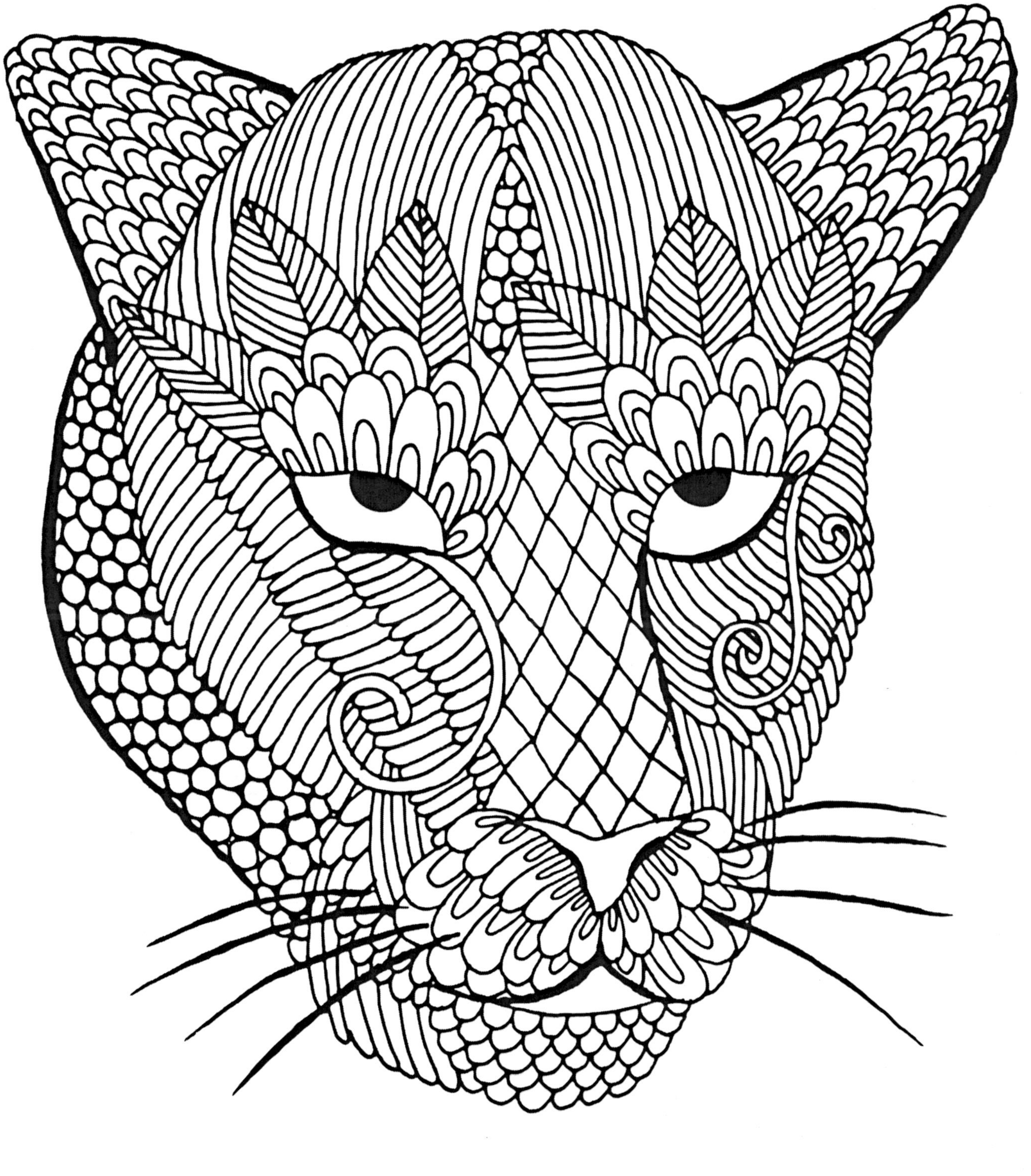

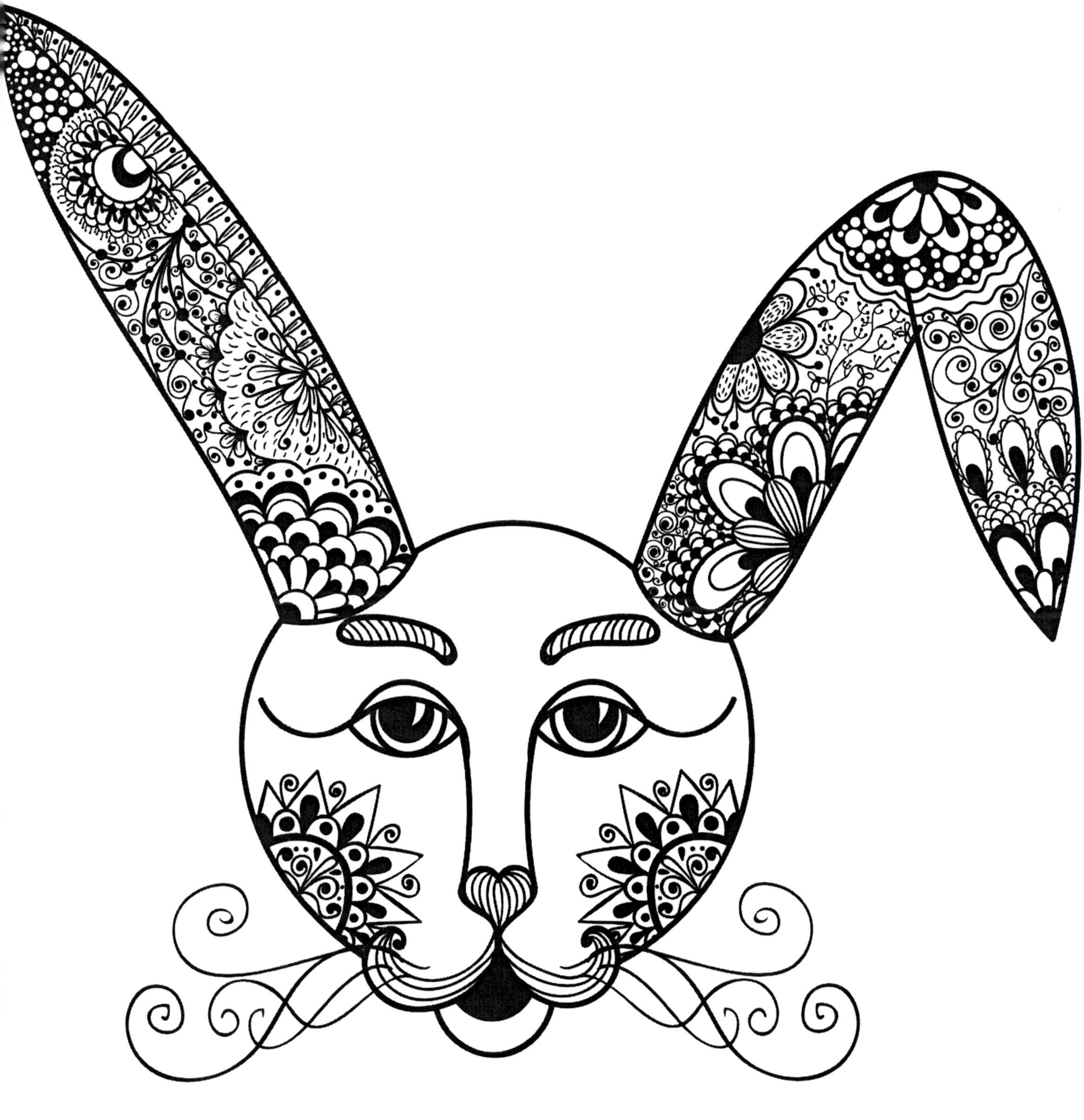

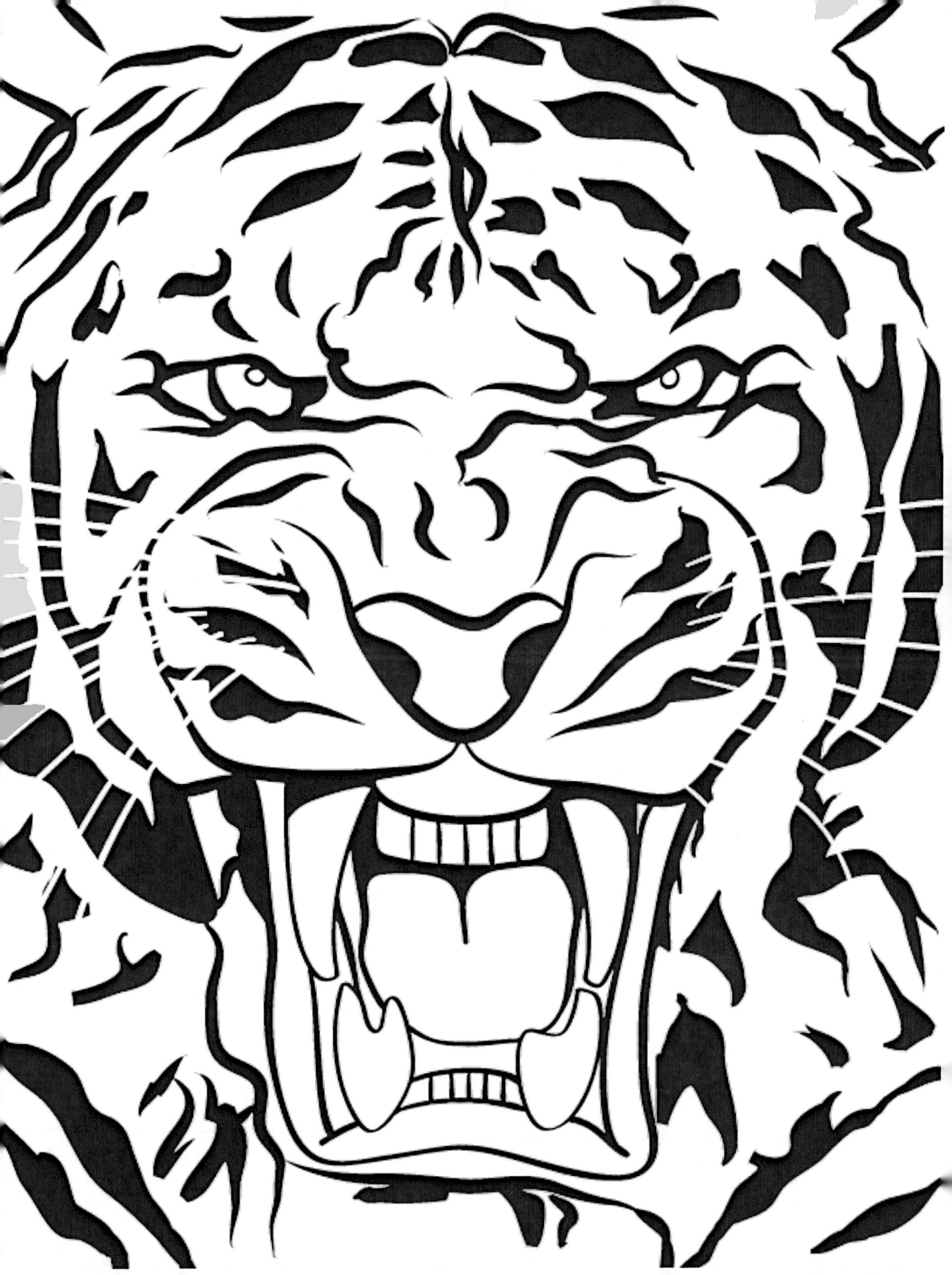

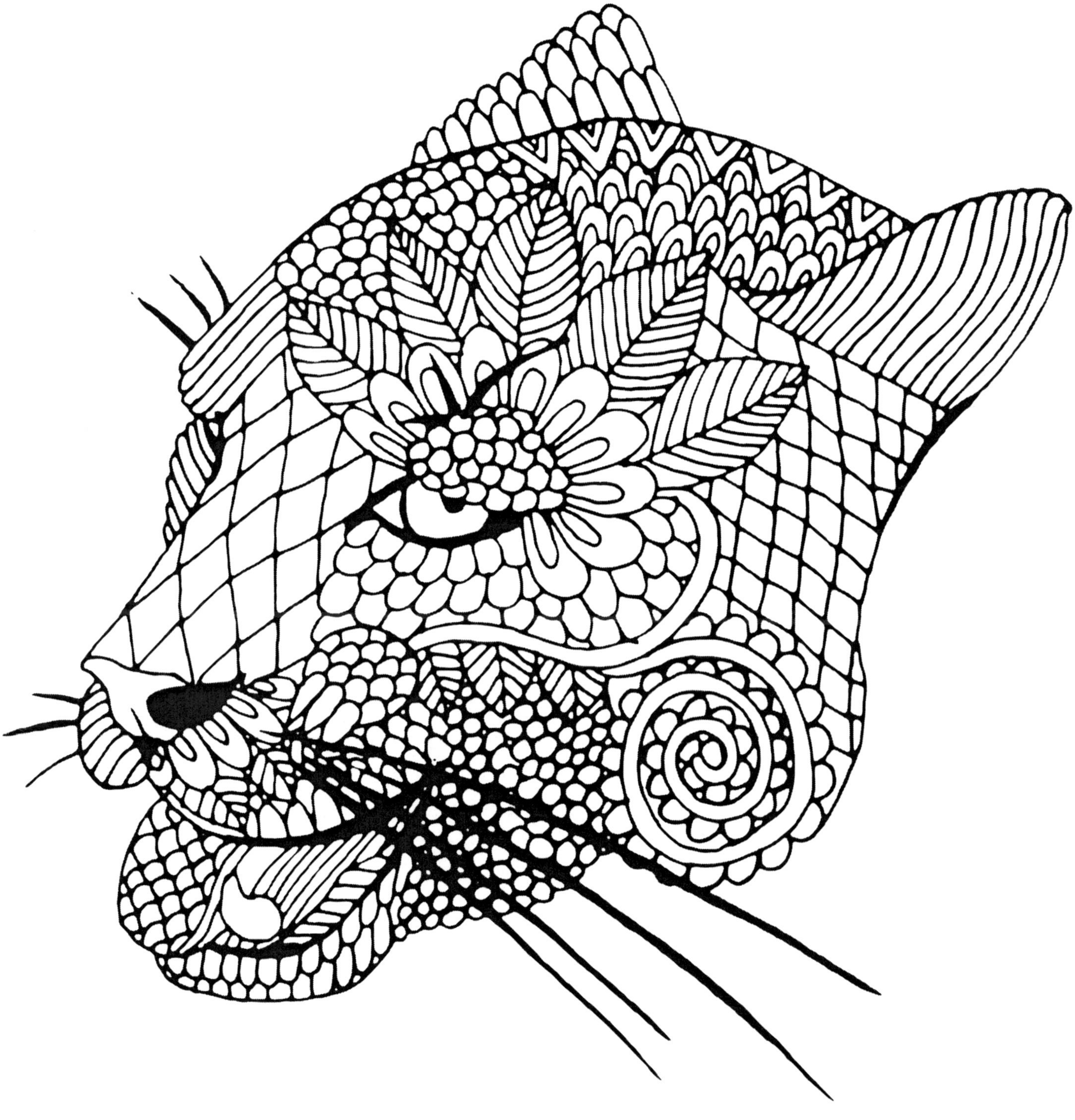

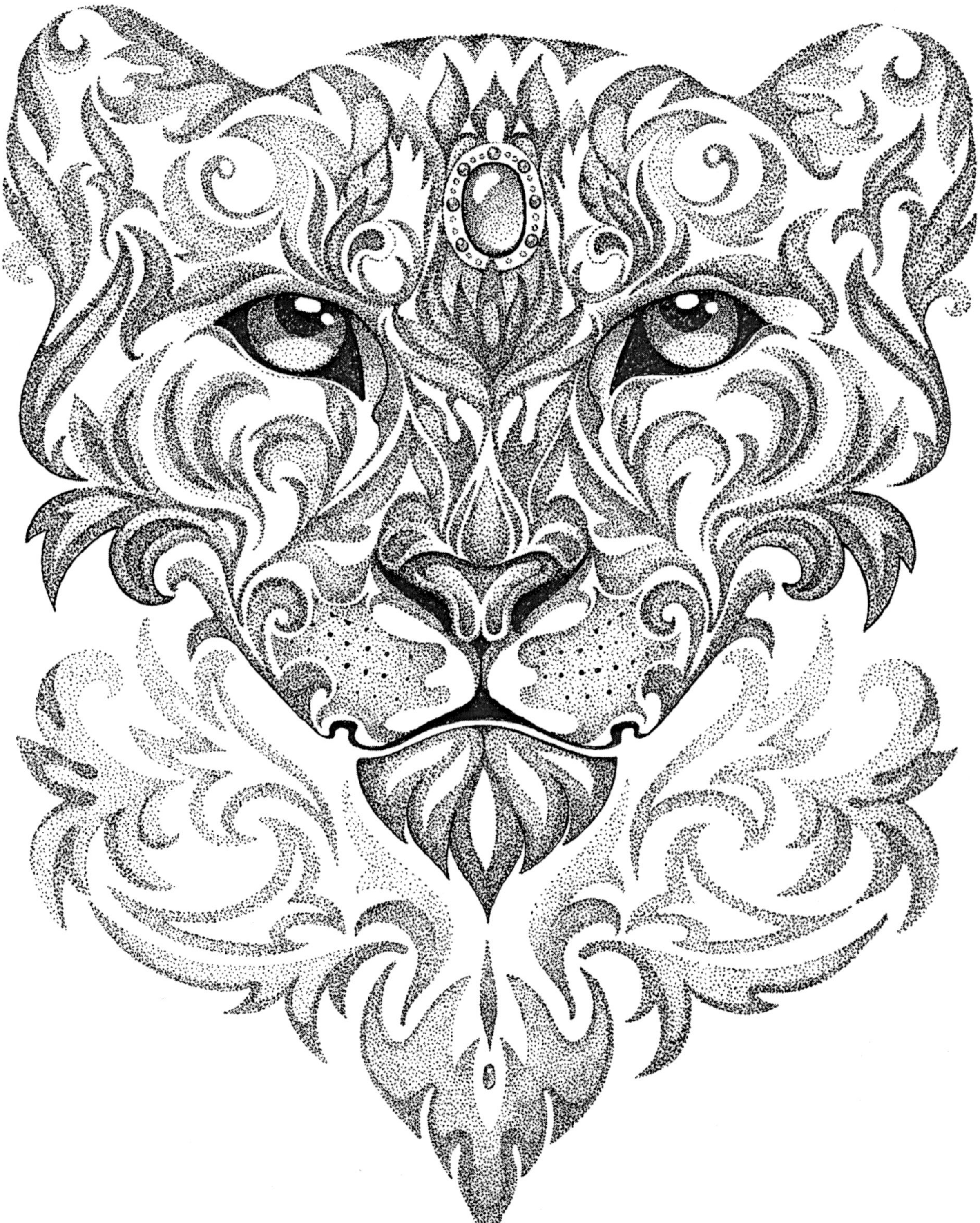

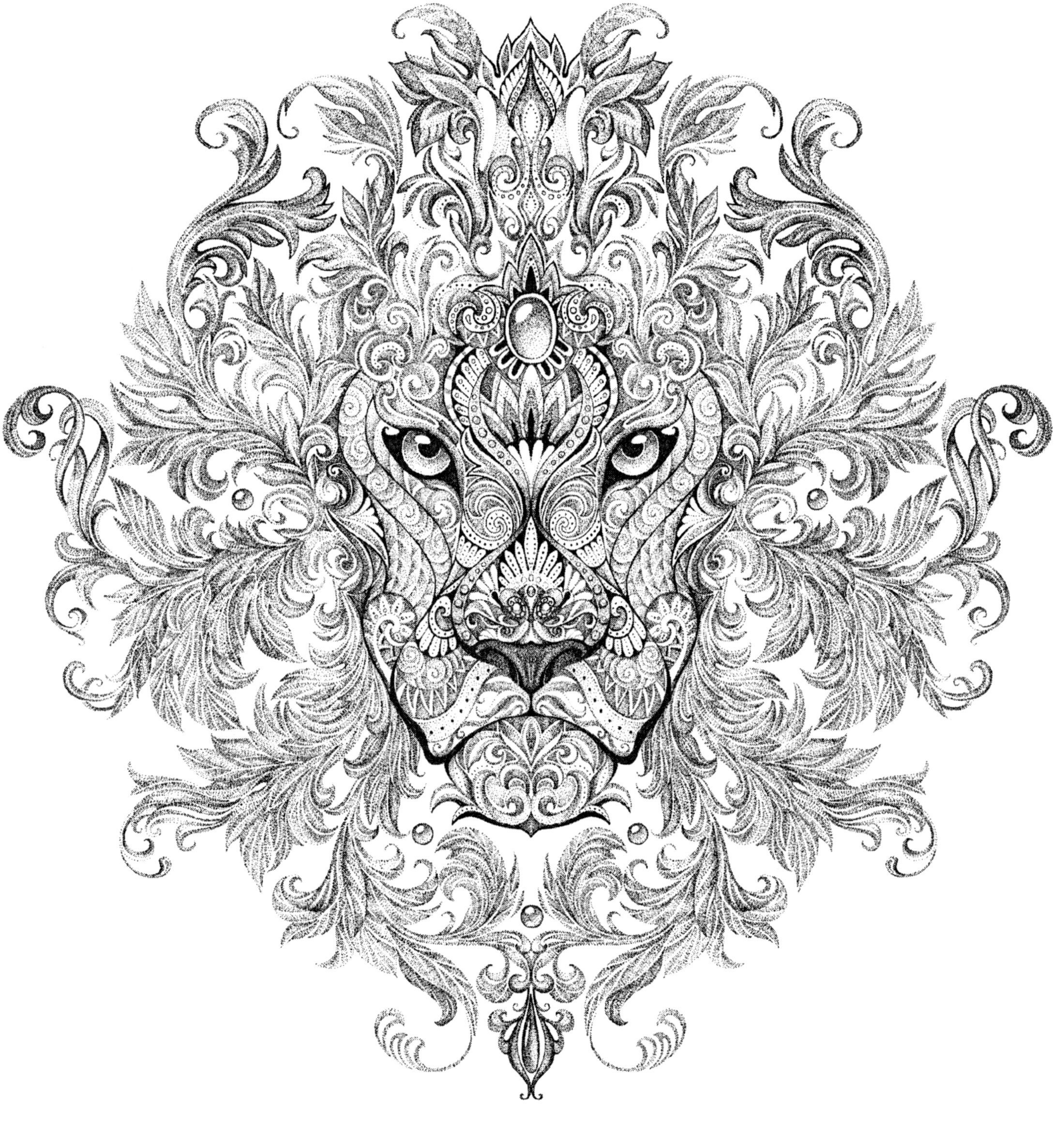

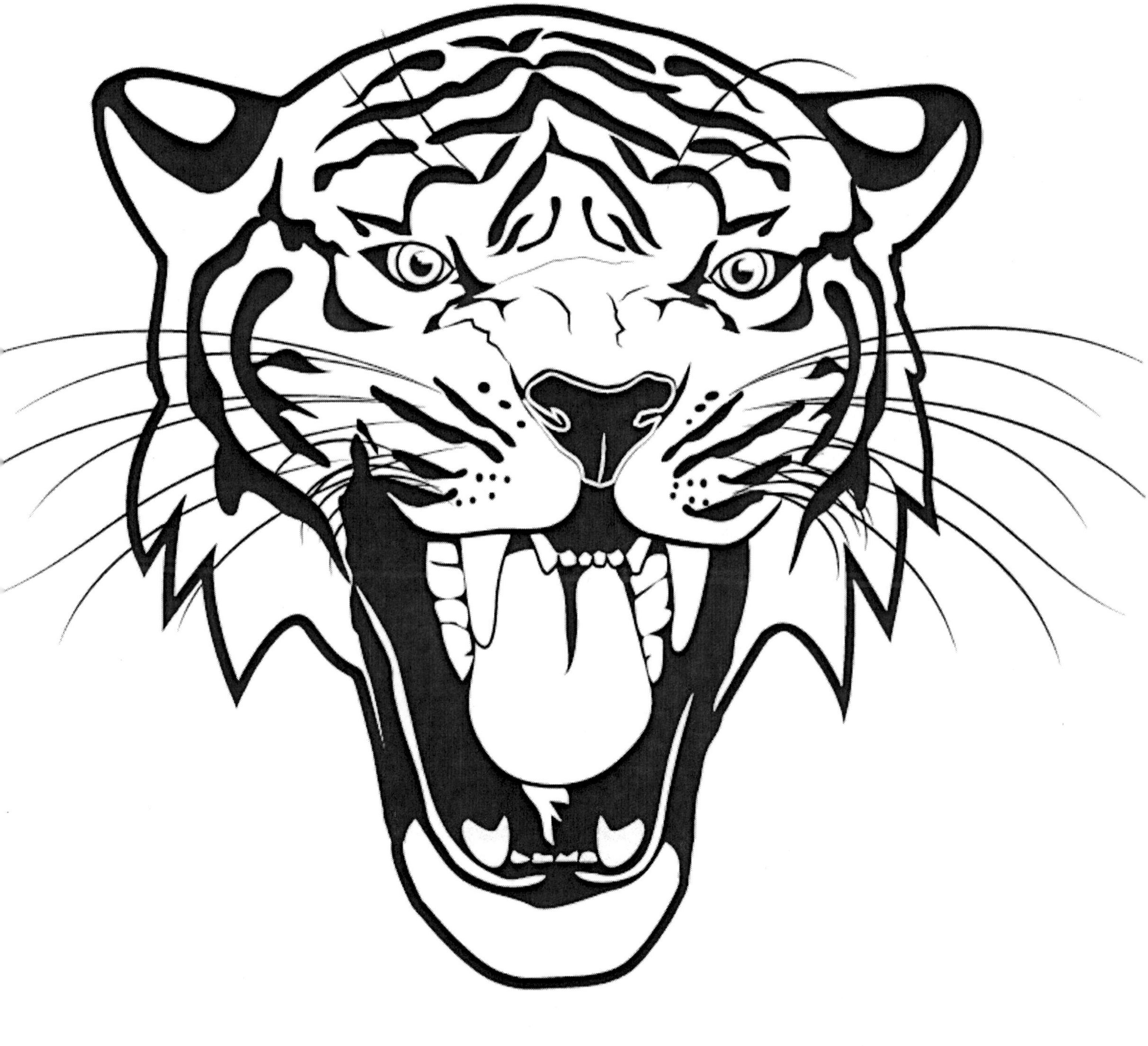

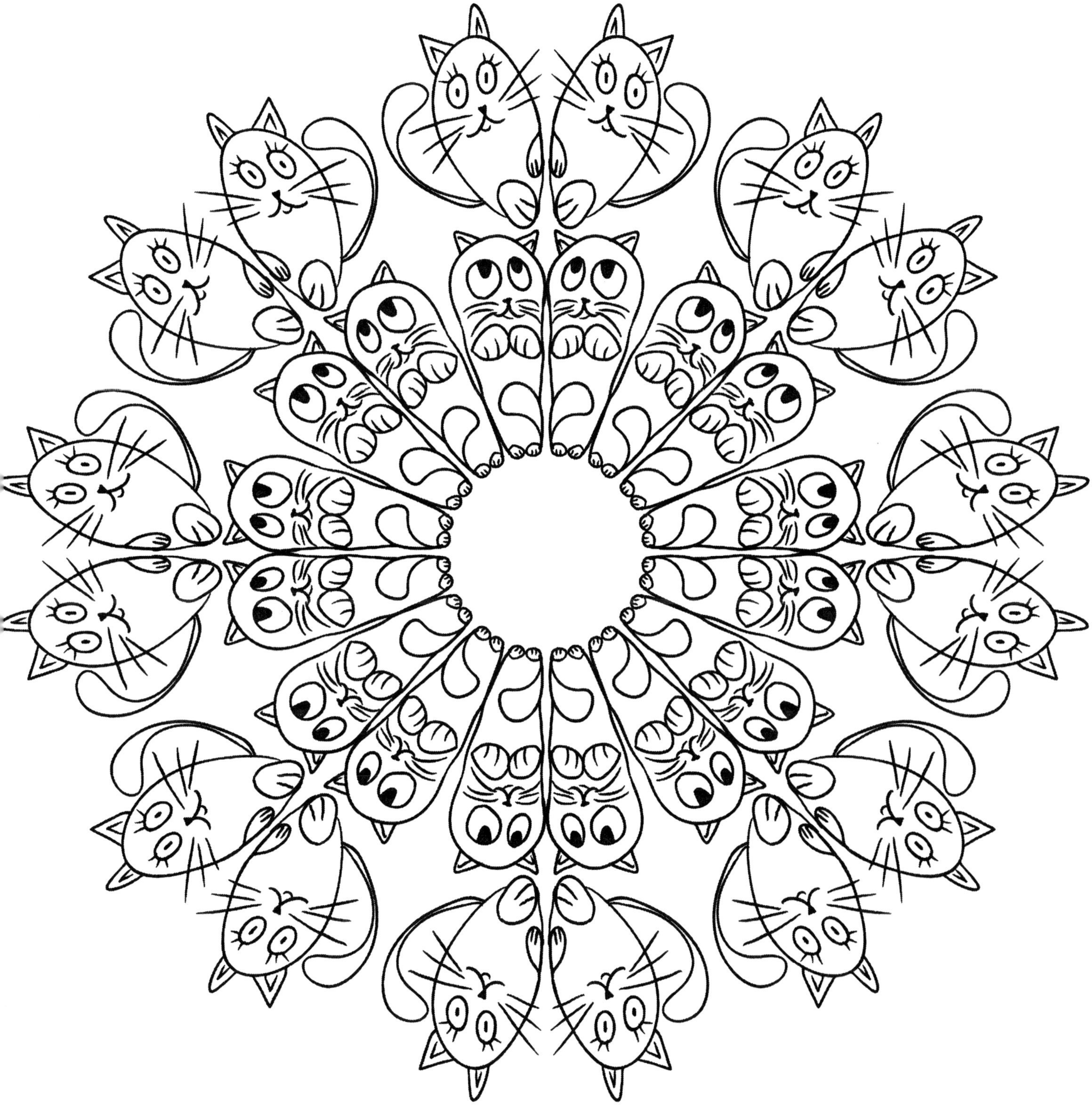

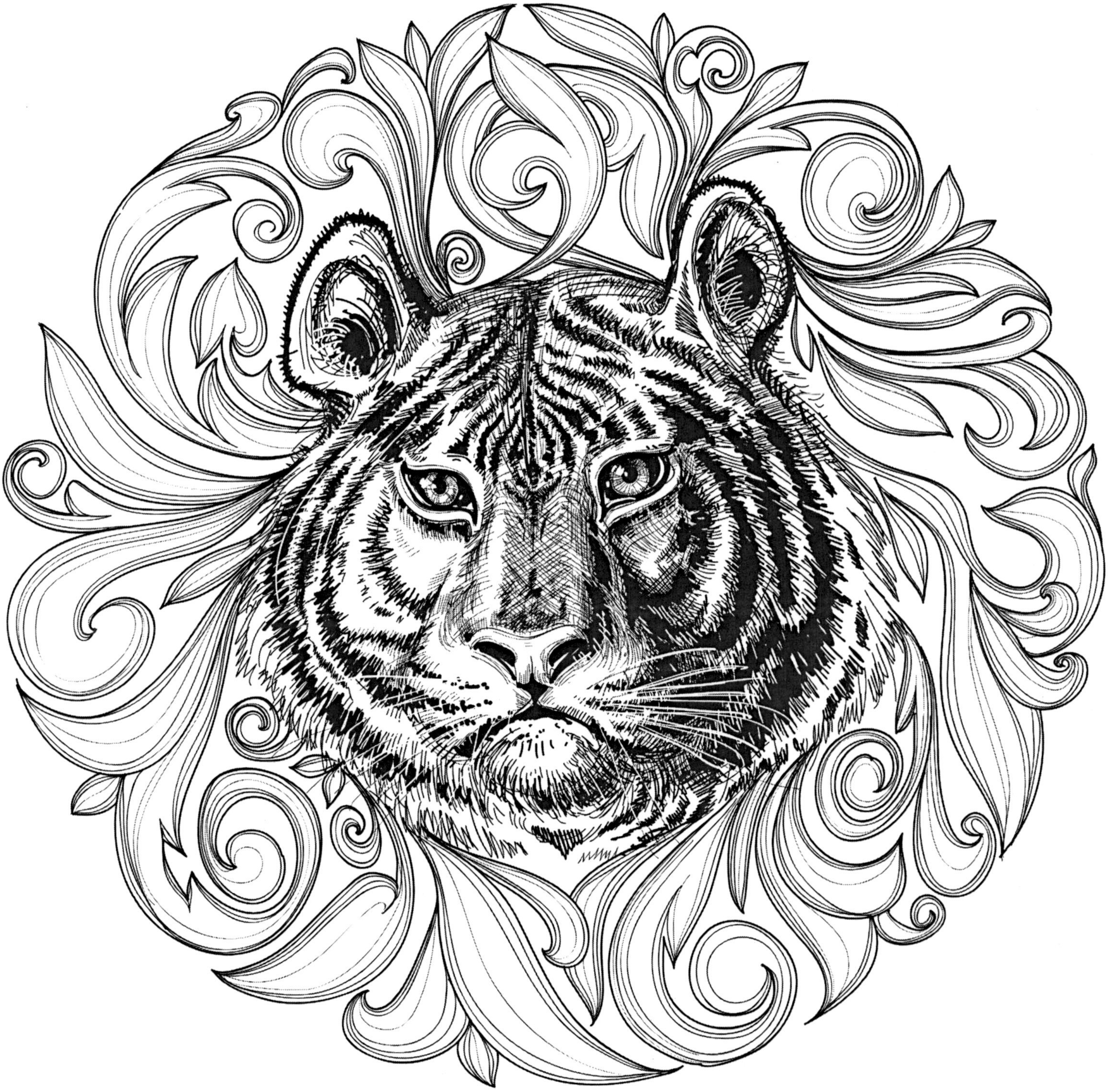

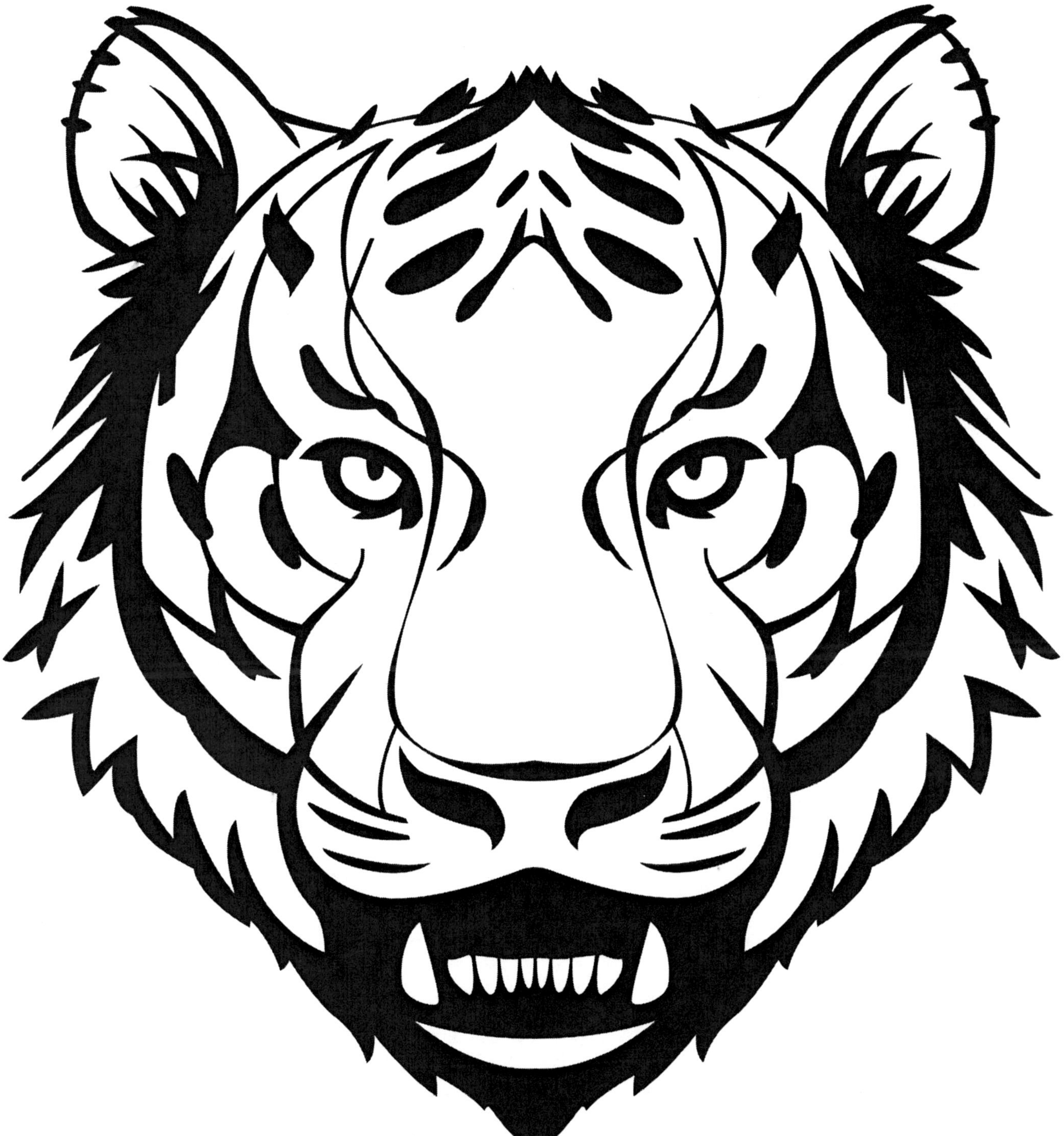

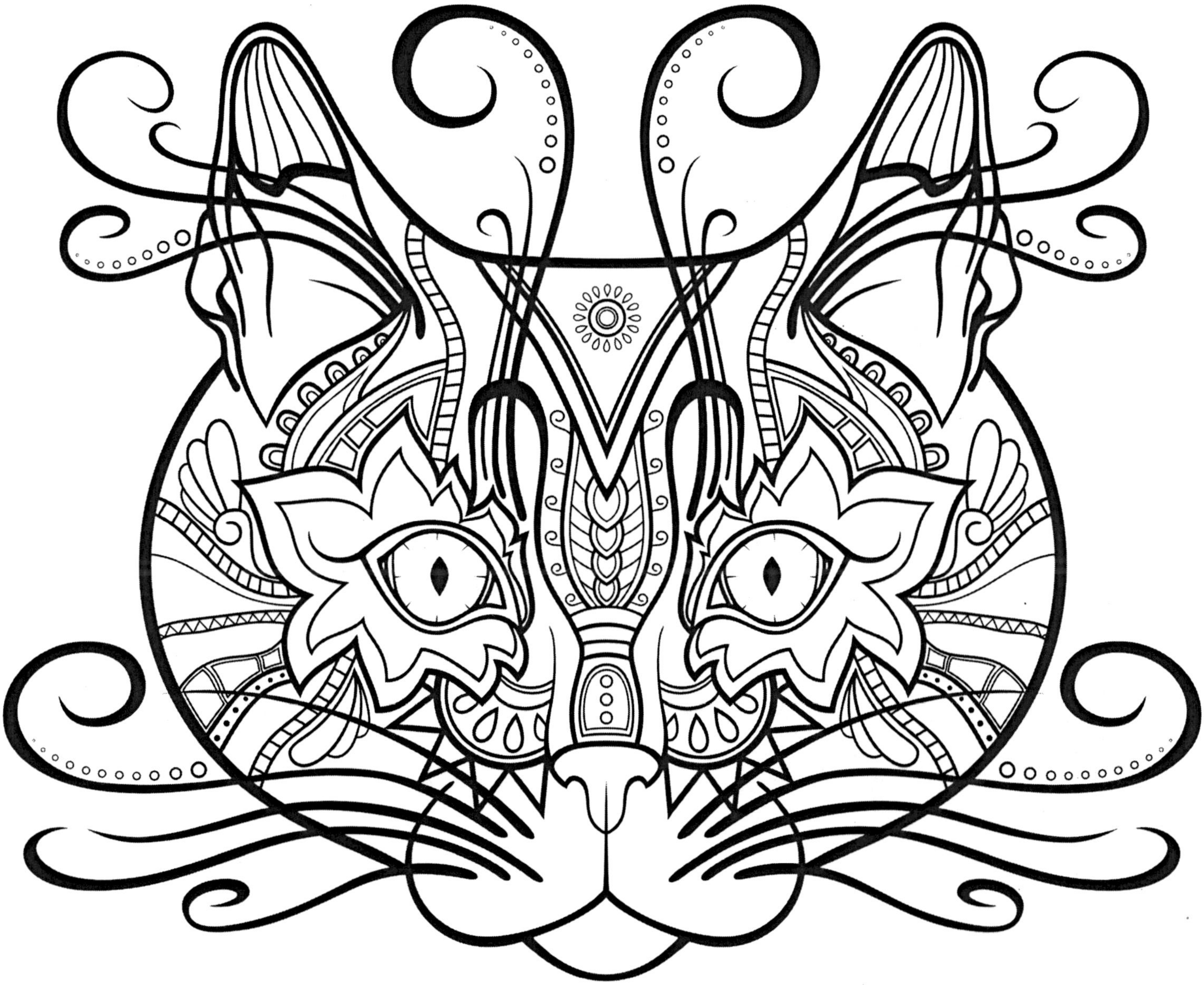

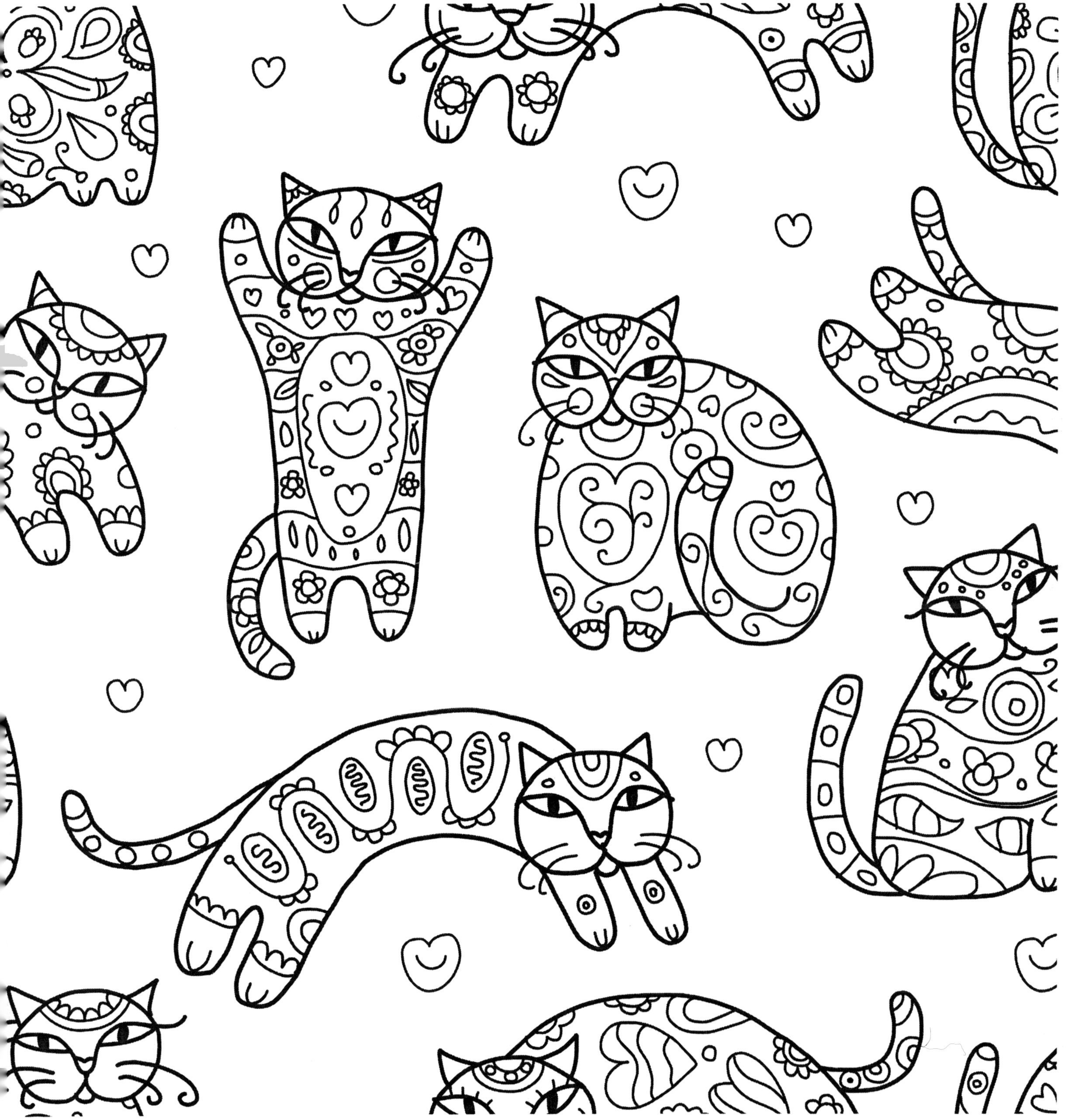

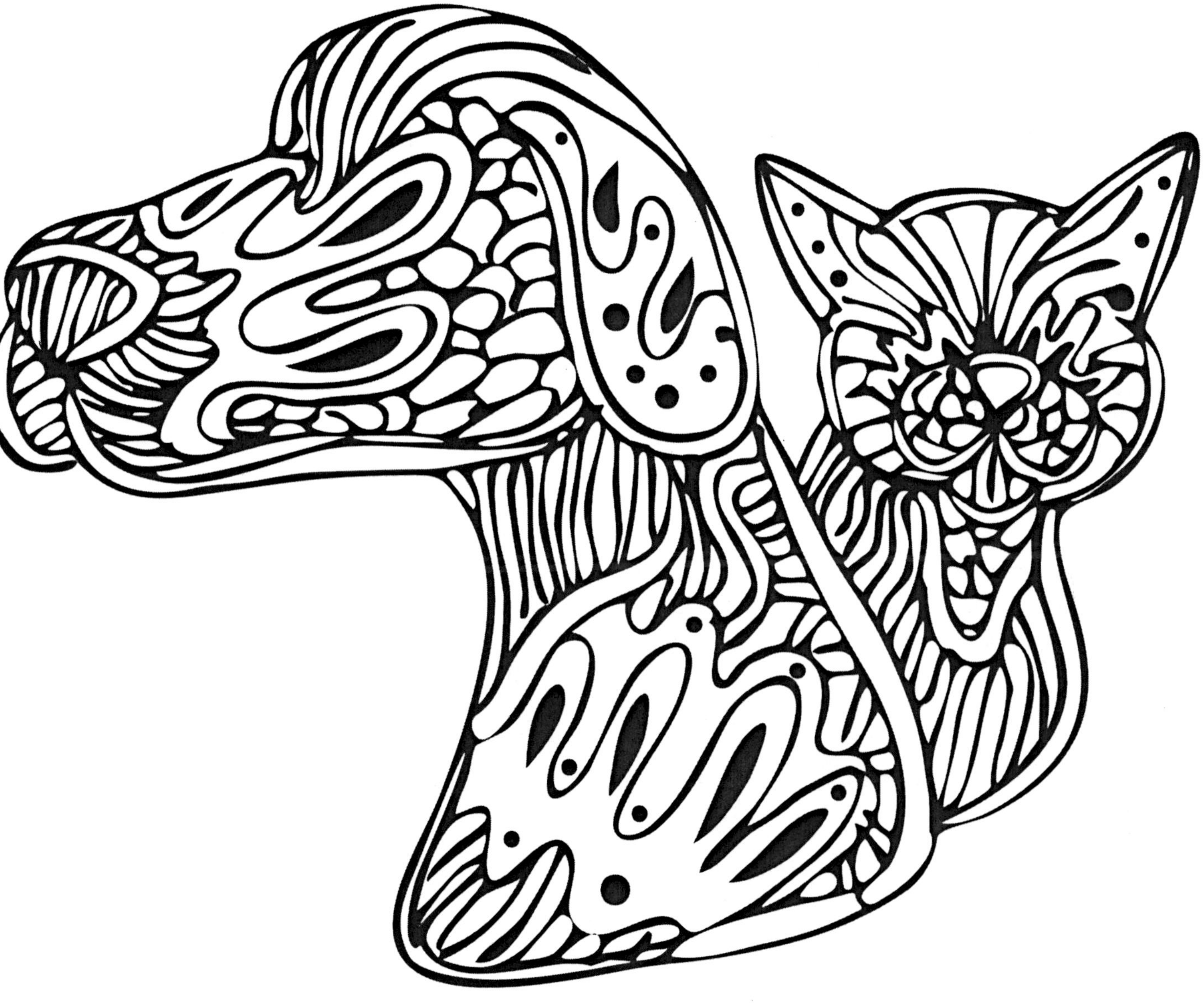

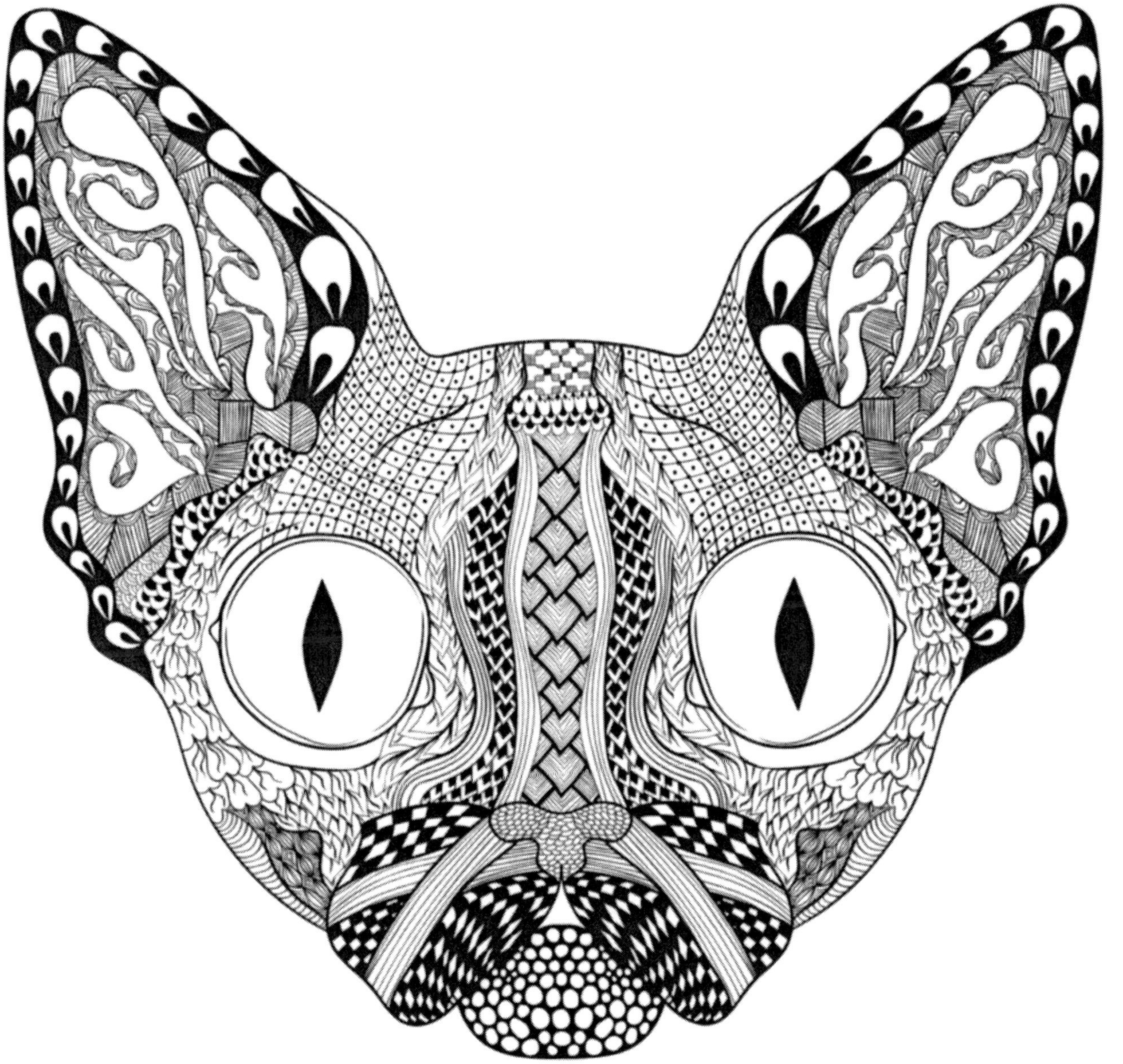

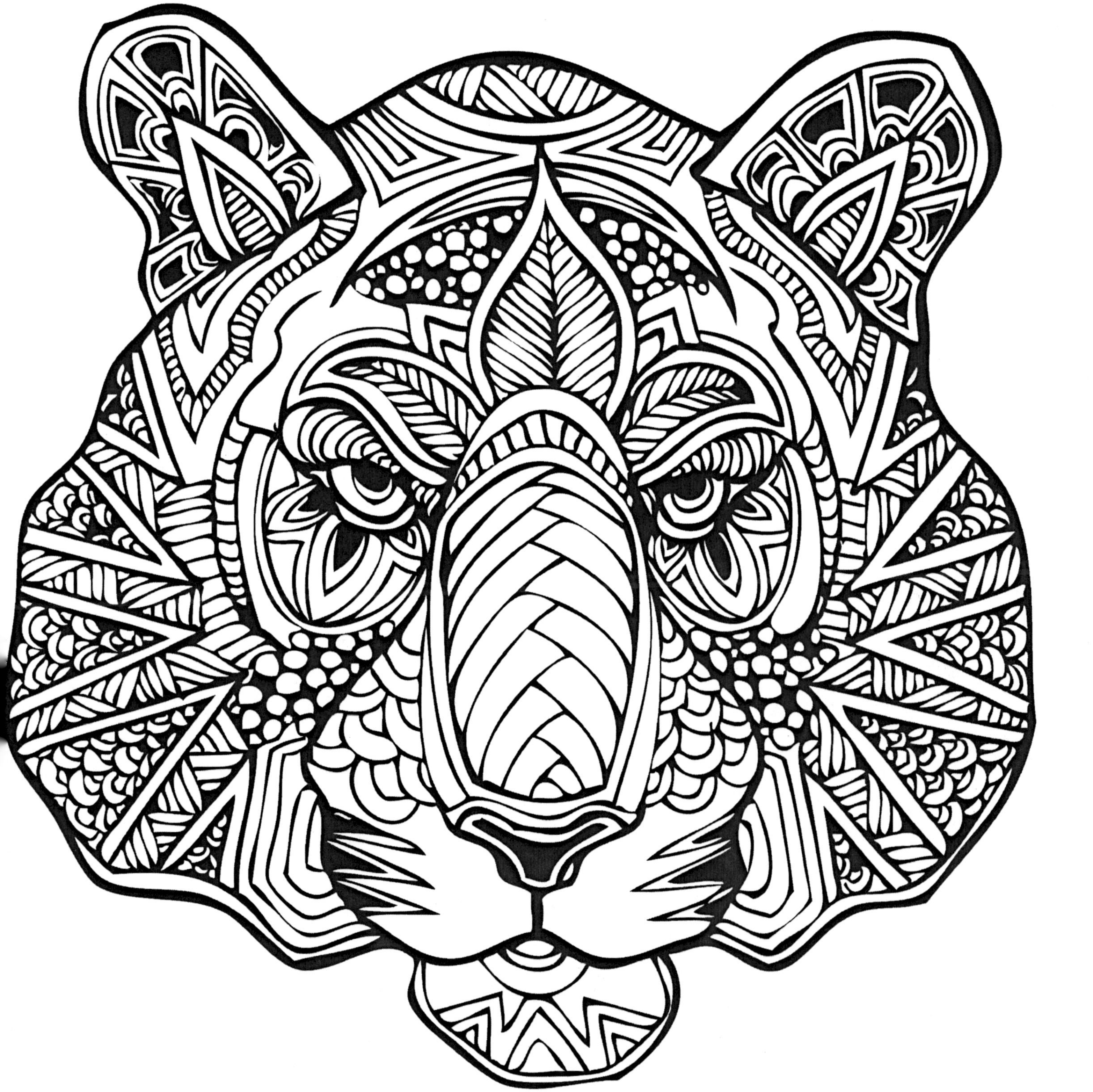

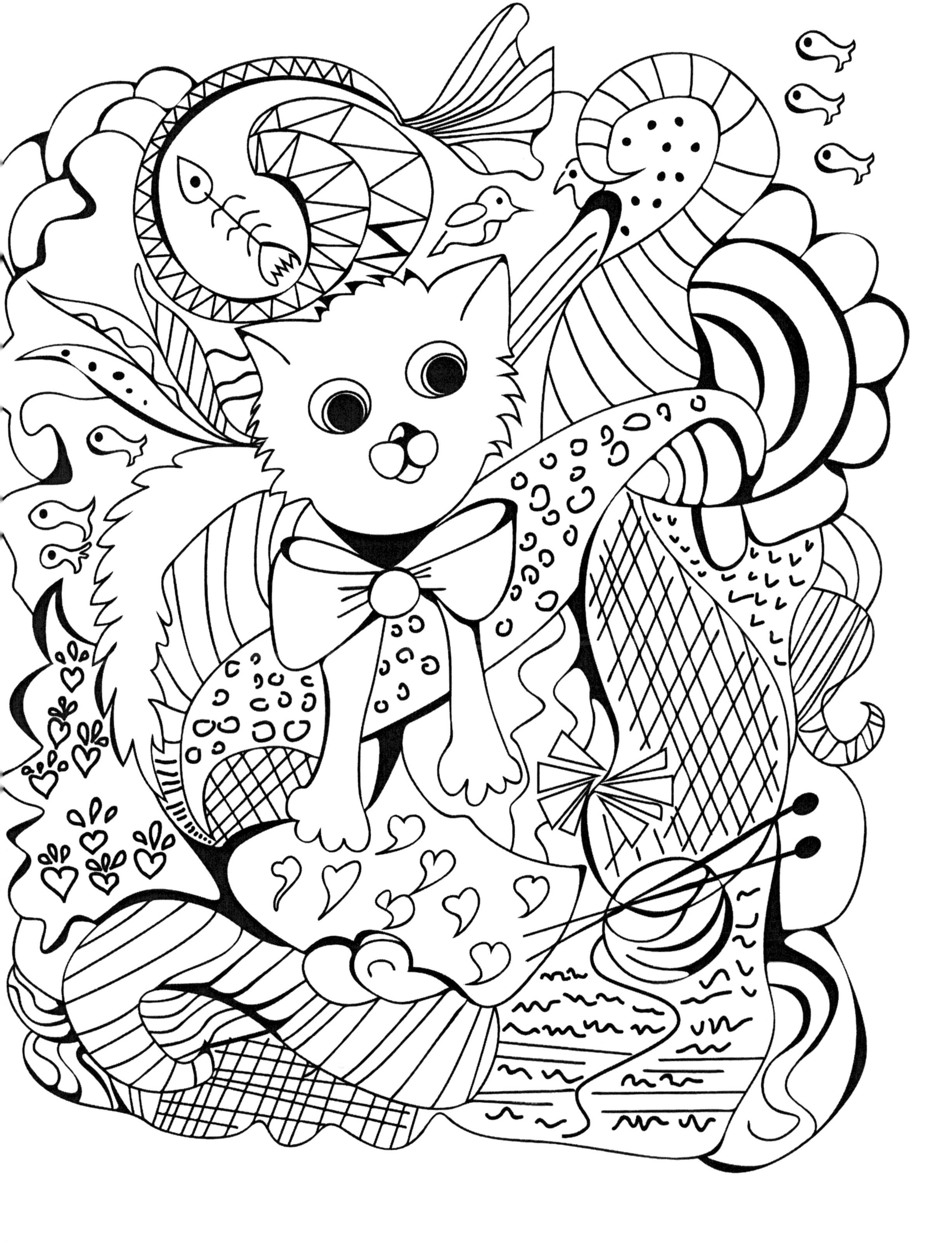

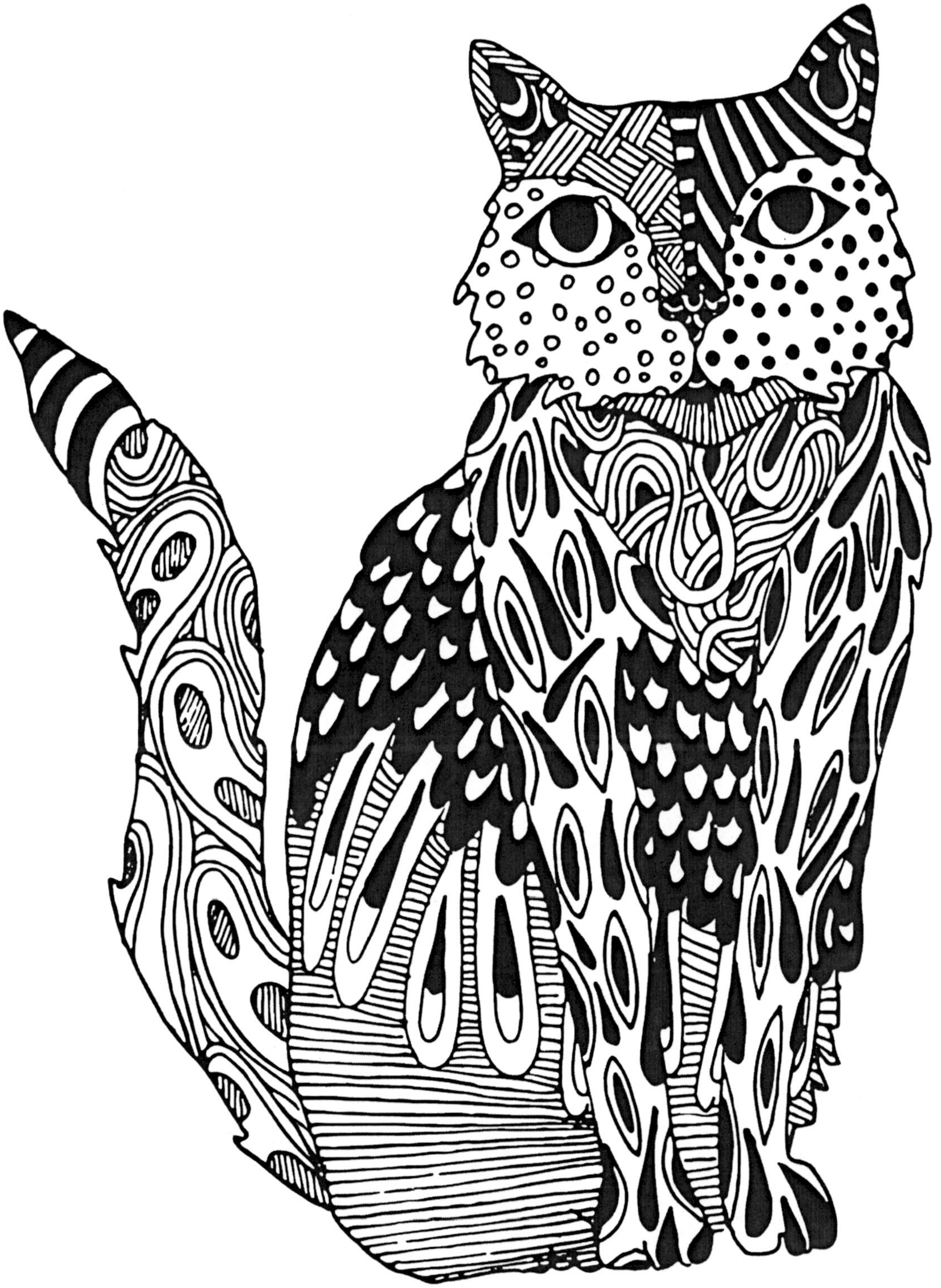

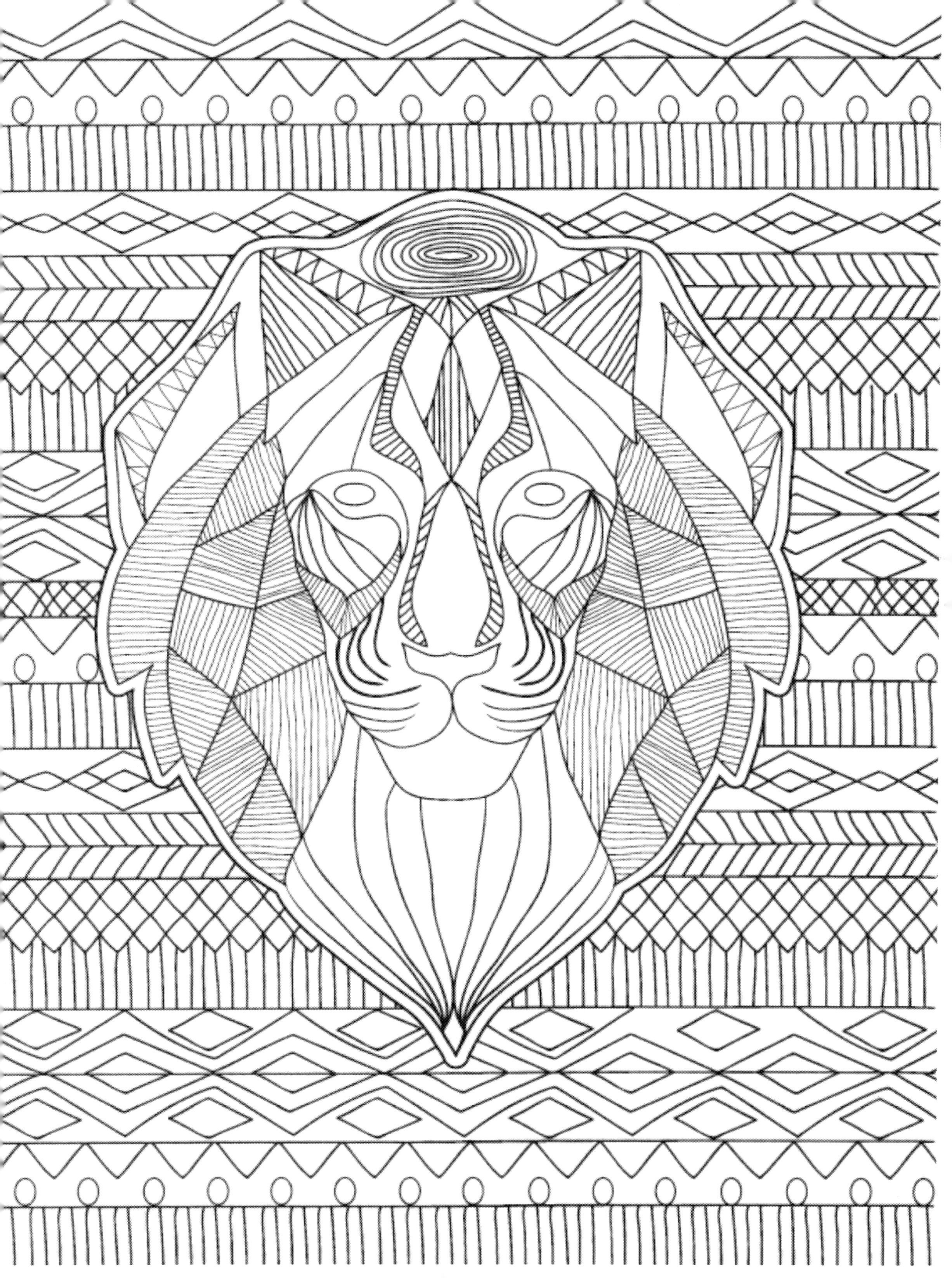

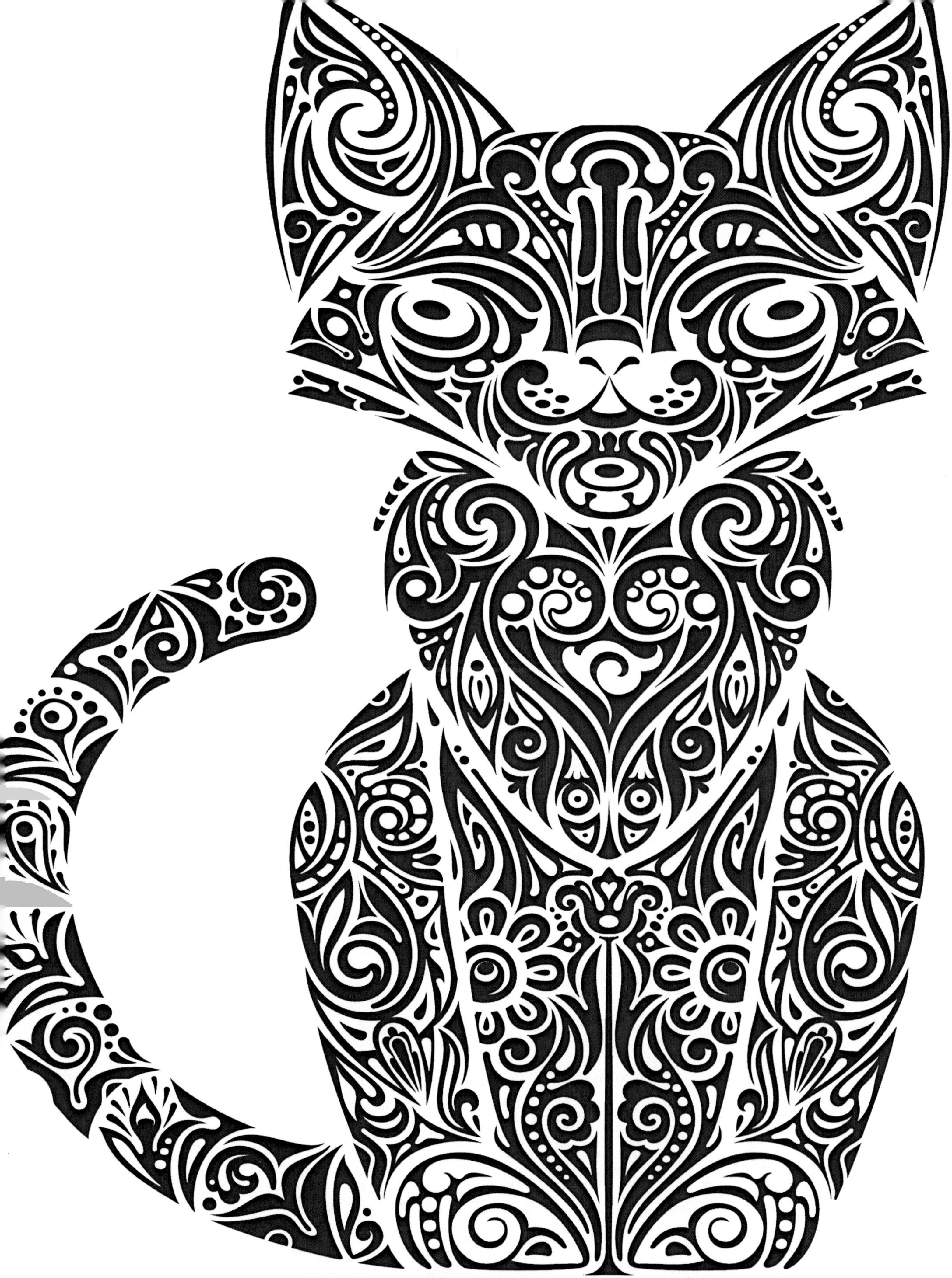

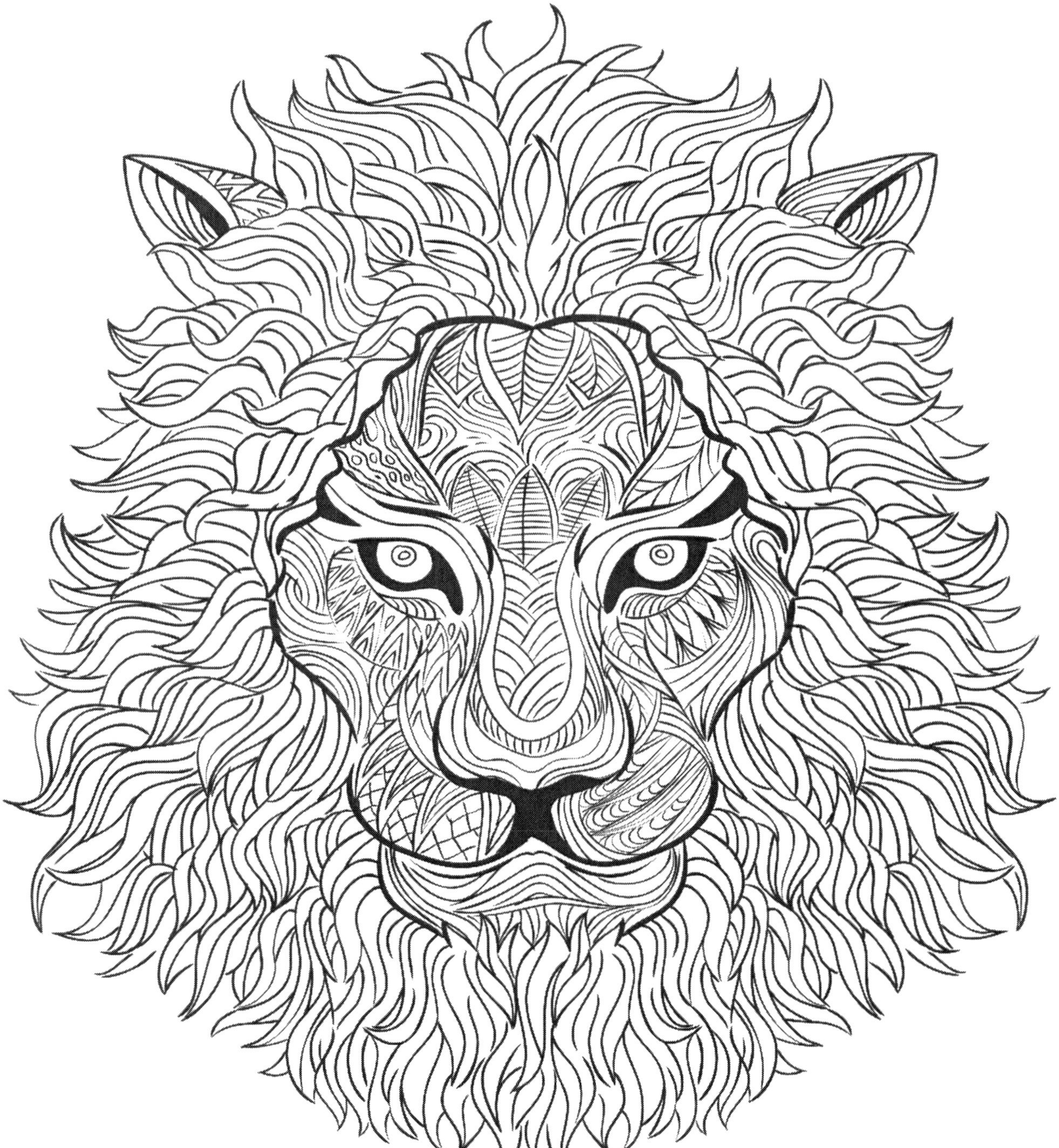

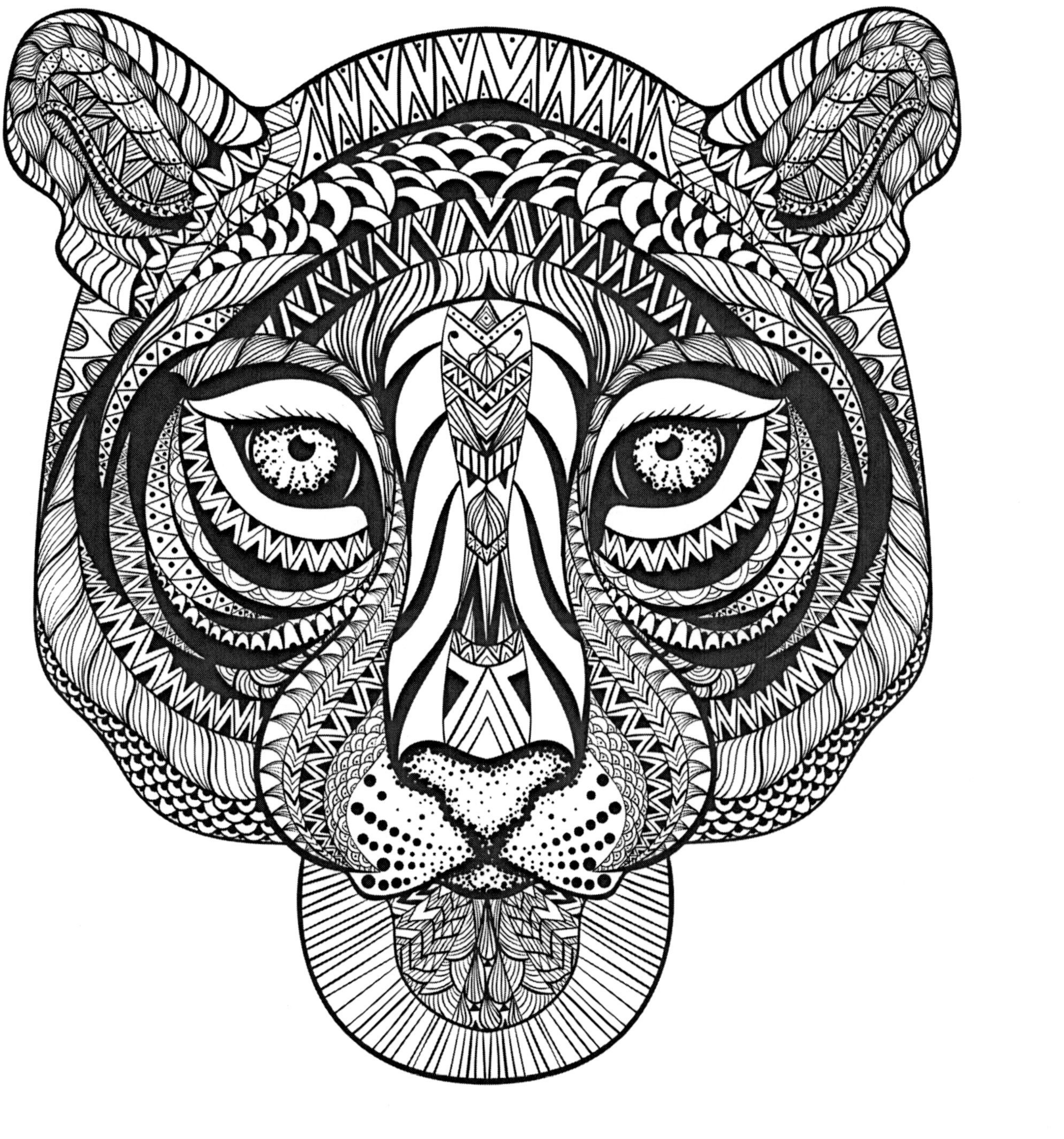

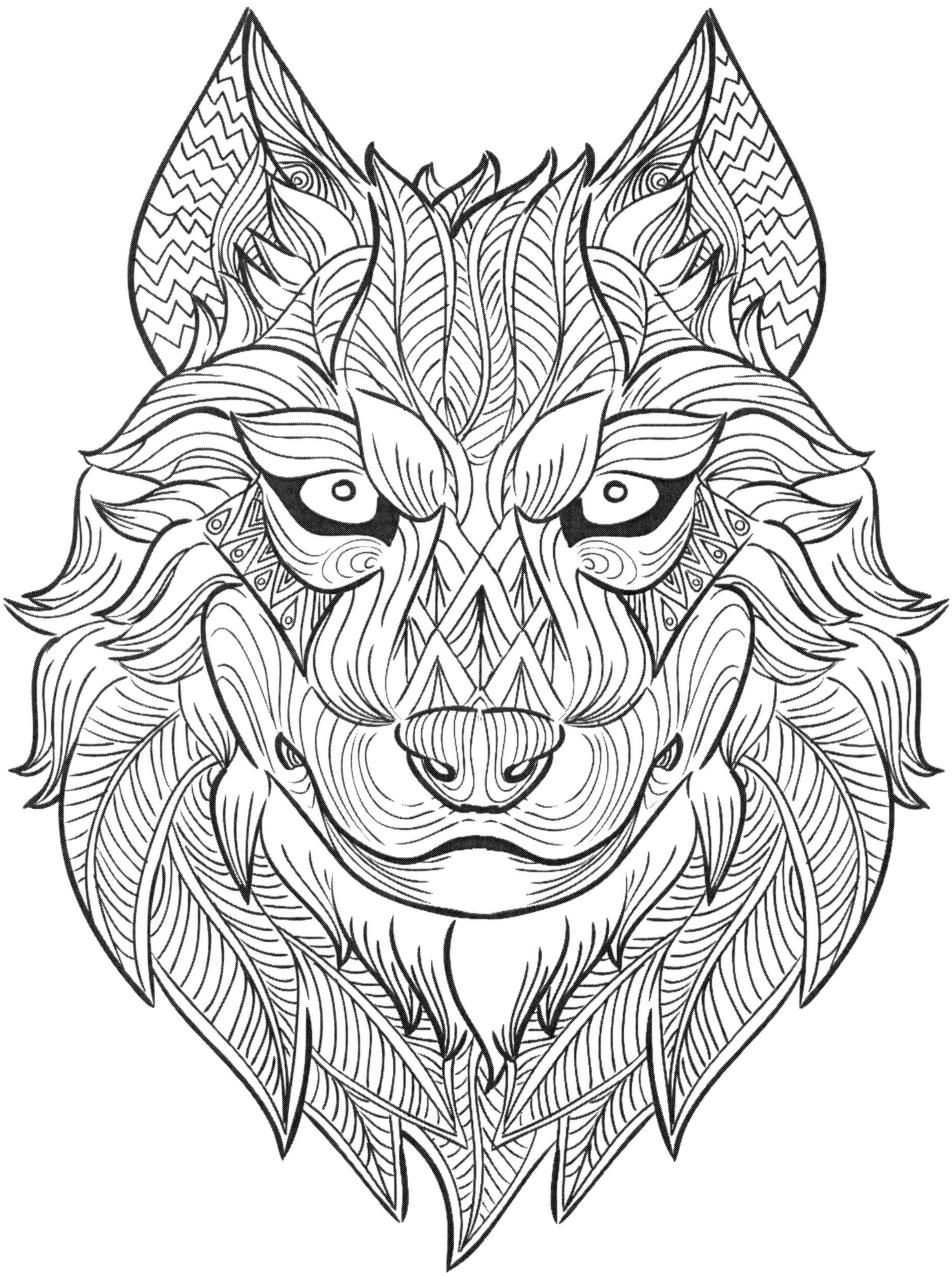

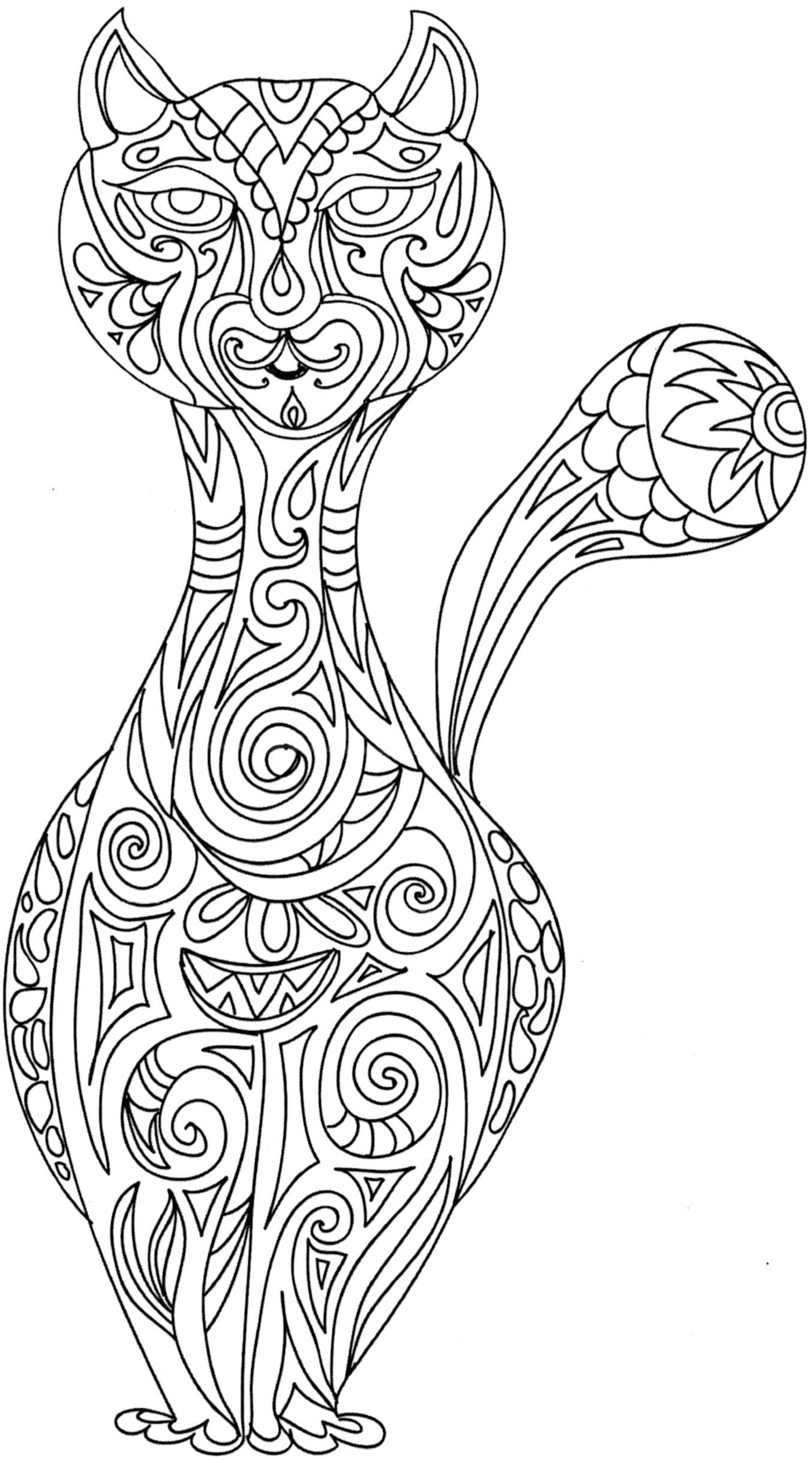

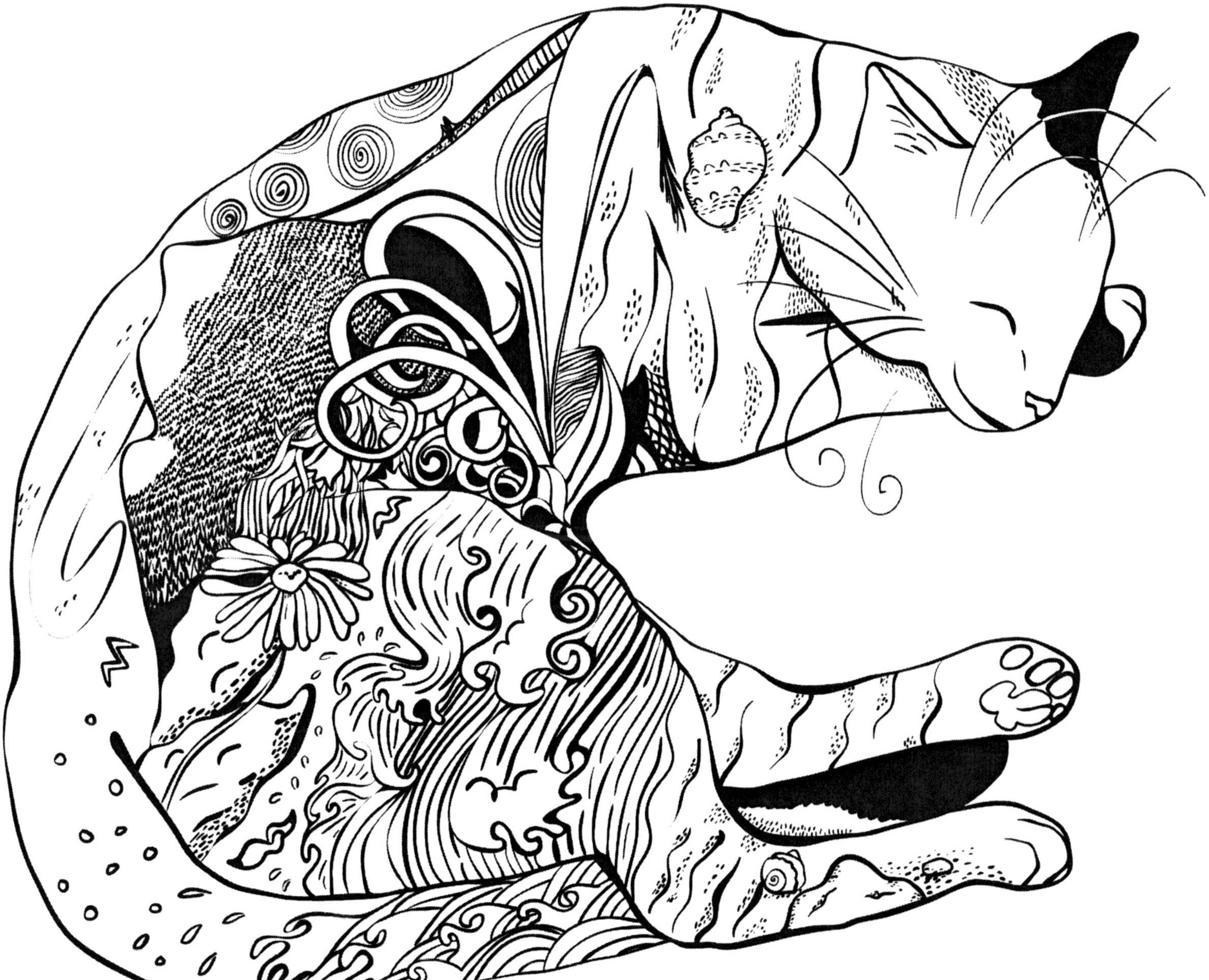

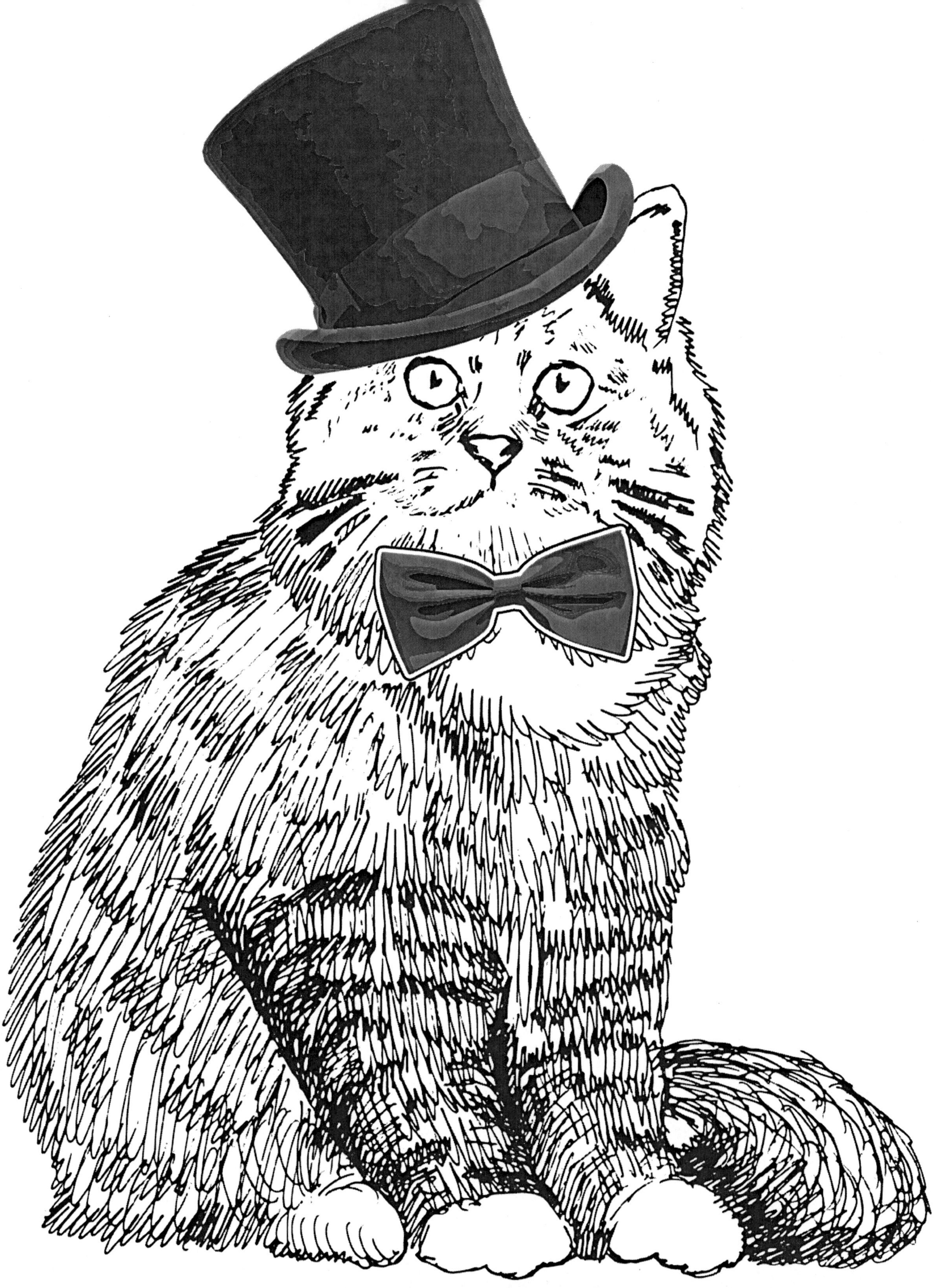

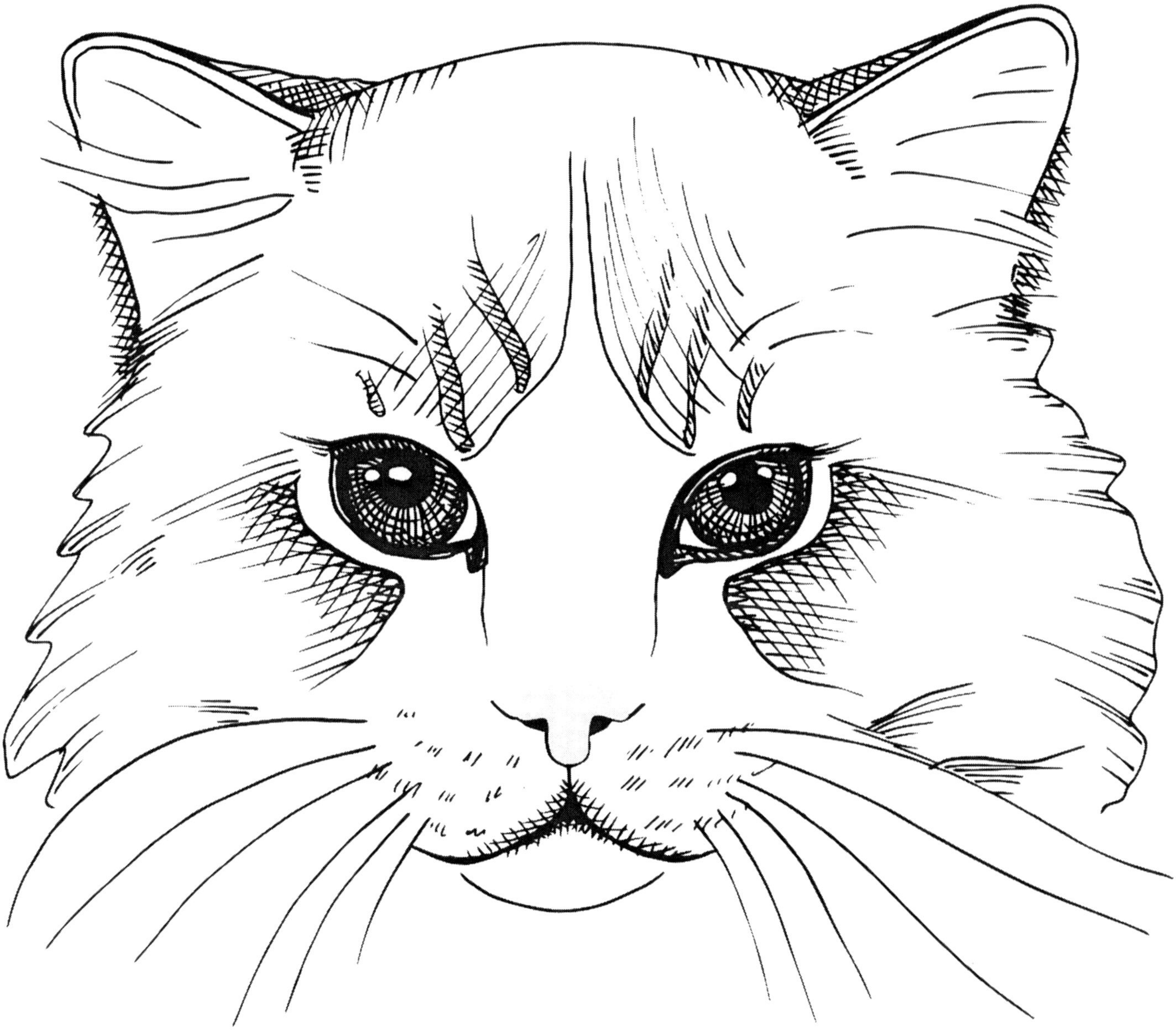

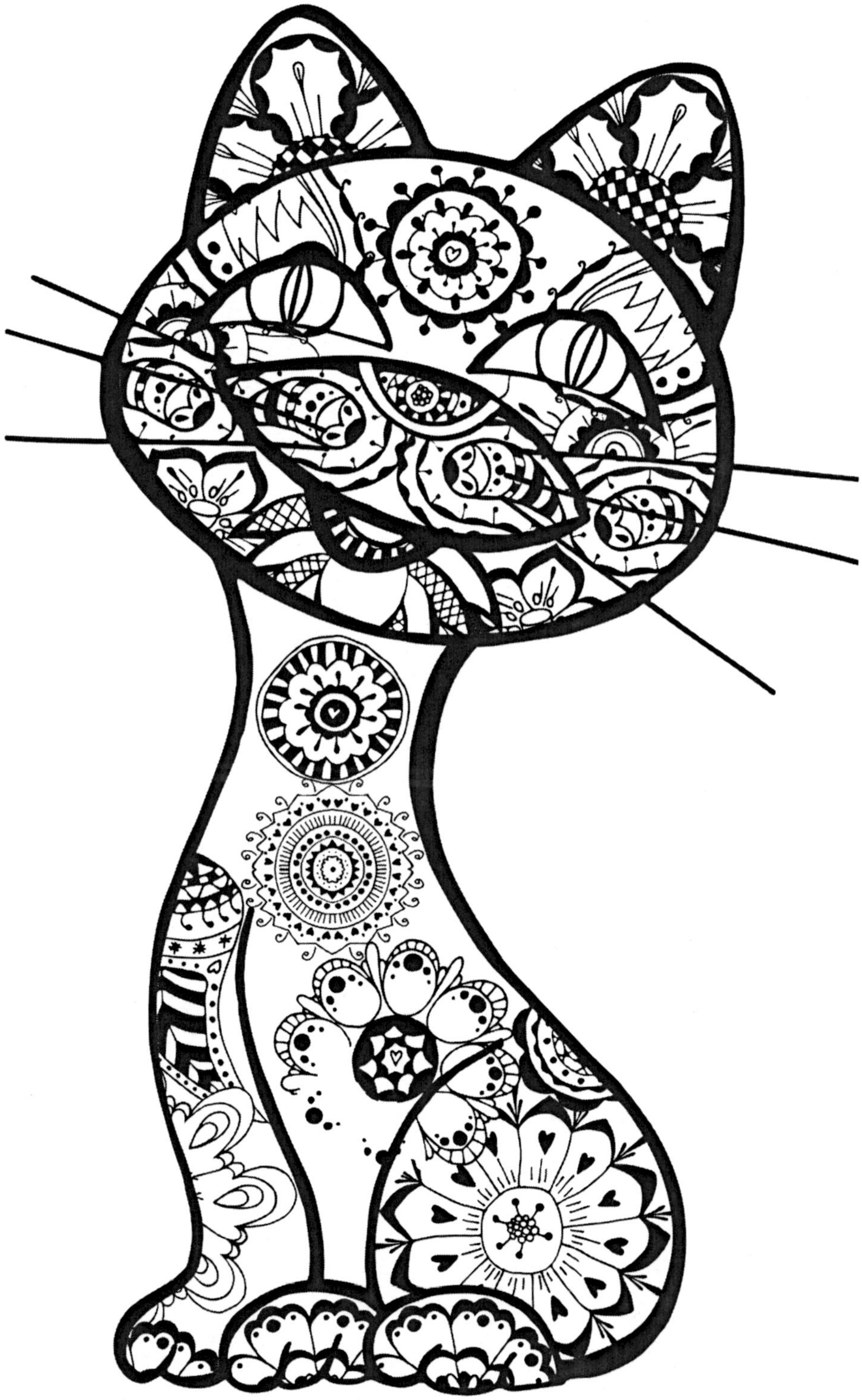

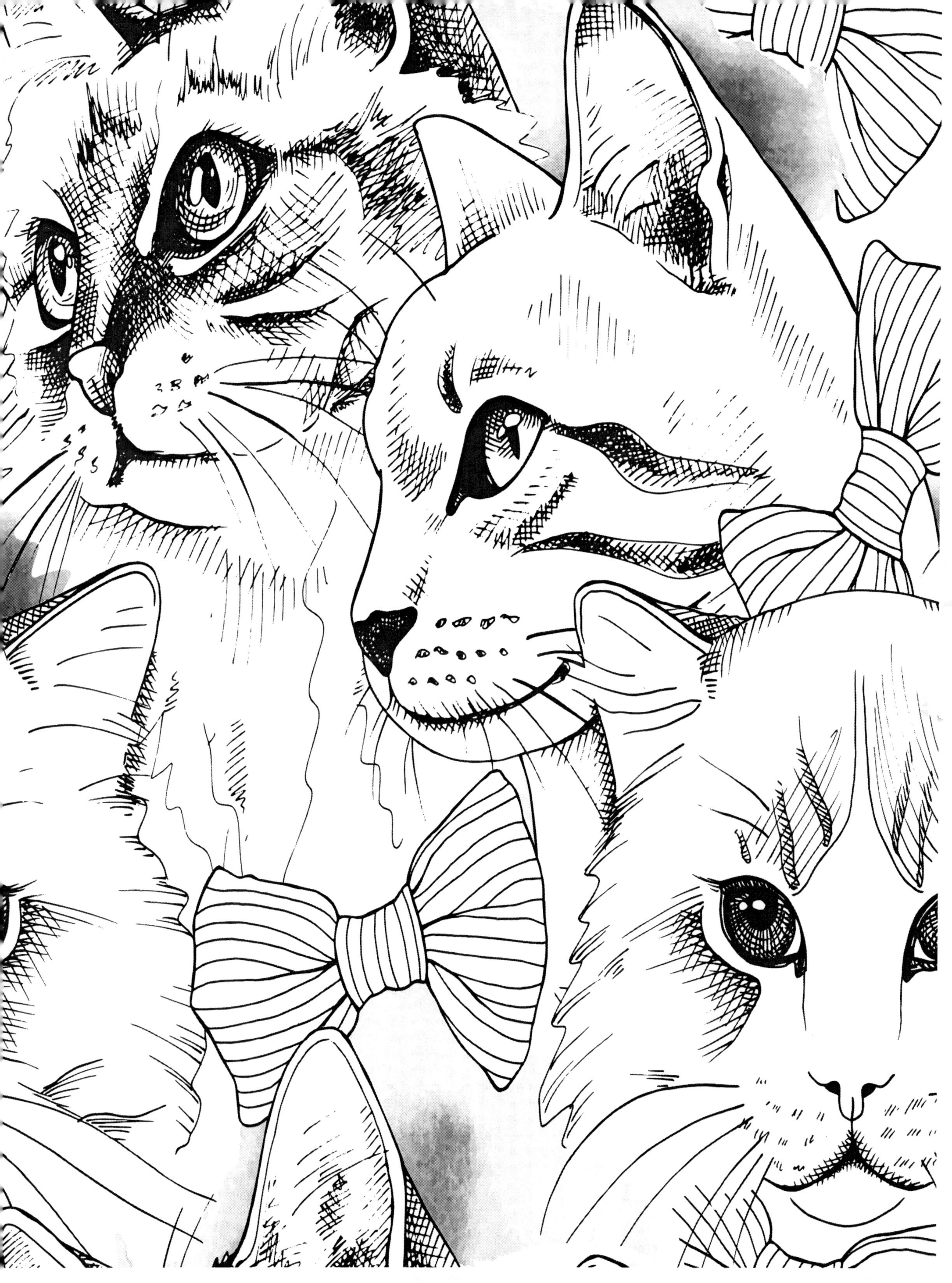

Thank You

If you enjoyed Coloring the Colorful Cats, please take a little time to share your thoughts and post a positive review with 5 star rating on Amazon, it would encourage me and make me serve you better. It'd Really be greatly appreciated.

We'll never be perfect, but that won't stop us from trying. Your feedback makes us serve you better. Send ideas, criticism, Compliment or anything else you think we should hear to info@adultscoloringartist.com. We'll Reply you As soon as we receive your Mail. :)

Visit our Author Page to get More Amazing Adults Coloring Books HERE›› https://www.amazon.com/author/adultcoloringbooksbestsellers

CPSIA information can be obtained at www.ICGtesting.com
Printed in the USA
LVOW09s1231240116
472053LV00014B/326/P